CHARLES ALBERT COLLMAN

Our Mysterious
PANICS
1830-1930

A
STORY OF
EVENTS AND
THE MEN
INVOLVED

Martino Publishing
Mansfield Centre CT
2009

Martino Publishing
P.O. Box 373,
Mansfield Centre, CT 06250 USA

web-site: www.martinopublishing.com

ISBN-13: 978-1-57898-786-3 (hardcover : alk. paper)
ISBN-10: 1-57898-786-5 (hardcover : alk. paper)
ISBN-13: 978-1-57898-787-0 (softcover : alk. paper)
ISBN-10: 1-57898-787-3 (softcover : alk. paper)

© 2009 Martino Publishing

Library of Congress Cataloging-in-Publication Data

Collman, Charles Albert, b. 1868.
Our mysterious panics, 1830-1930: a story of events and the men
involved.
    p. cm.
Includes index.
ISBN-13: 978-1-57898-786-3 (hardcover : alk. paper)
ISBN-10: 1-57898-786-5 (hardcover : alk. paper)
ISBN-13: 978-1-57898-787-0 (softcover : alk. paper)
ISBN-10: 1-57898-787-3 (softcover : alk. paper)
1. Depressions. 2. Depressions--1929--United States. 3. Financial
crises. 4. Curiosities and wonders. 5. Speculation. I. Title.

HB3743.C65 2009
338.5'42--dc22   2009028526

Cover Design T. Matarazzo

Printed in the United States of America On 100% Acid-Free Paper

CHARLES ALBERT COLLMAN

Our Mysterious

PANICS

1830-1930

A
STORY OF
EVENTS AND
THE MEN
INVOLVED

19   31

NEW YORK

WILLIAM MORROW & CO.

Published, January, 1931
Second Printing, March, 1931

PRINTED IN THE U. S. A. BY
QUINN & BODEN COMPANY, INC.
RAHWAY, N. J.

"And it is not a problem in academic economics. It is a great human problem. The margin of shrinkage brings loss of savings, unemployment, privation, hardship and fear, which are no part of our ideals for the American economic system."

—From President Hoover's address to the American Bankers' Association, Cleveland, October 2, 1930.

"Men do not make panics deliberately; they are their unconscious agents."—*Our Mysterious Panics.*

CONTENTS

vii

Contents

INTRODUCTION

INTRODUCTION

ONCE again, in its century of sprightly annals, we have been called upon to puzzle our brains over the operation of the great financial arena, in which America's capital pits itself against the world. After generations of theories, hypotheses and postulates, our economists to-day are still at odds over the cause of that familiar apparition, the Panic. The confusion in views expressed by Wall Street's financiers and financial authorities, as to the origin of the disasters of the autumn of 1929, shows that the Street is no clearer in mind on this subject than are the craftsmen of the Dismal Science.

The need for delving into the causes of the late unpleasantness has been quickened by the drab aftermath of its consequences, strung out beyond the trying year of 1930; so many telltale truths have come to light, so many confessions and disclosures. Even some of our friends, the solid underwriters, threw away caution in stimulating share values through their securities affiliates. And what a number of Wall Street playboys were caught at the business of mismanaging investment trusts! Disingenuous financiers jockeyed the stock market, customers' men de-

3

ceived their clients, absconders hit the dust and embezzlers were exposed. The State Bureau of Securities kept busy at the work of accusing—enjoining—prosecuting.

To be sure, in all the foregoing, Wall Street has merely demonstrated its age-old story,—ever new. To those who have watched the Street with reminiscent eyes, all these episodes are understandable and quite human.

In our boasted machine age, Wall Street is the most powerful of its machines; its function is to raise the money capital for the country's industries; but the methods by which we, boastedly the most practical-minded people on earth, go about this business, represent the nation's greatest economic waste.

Our optimisms and enthusiasms entangle us in panics, and these end in something still more disastrous,—the discouragement of thrift. This dénouement should decidedly give us all cause for reflection.

It may be wise for us to put aside those handbooks of the investment advisers; those textbooks, filled with the worldly unwisdom of the economic professors; those stock charts and tables of index-numbers, that relate only to past performances. Wise for us to forget the hollow-sounding predictions of the industrial captains, while trying to learn some

4

solid, elemental truths relating to a better understanding of Wall Street. Without passion or prejudice, we might attempt to penetrate that yet un-
disclosed secret,—the meaning of panic.

Yes, what are panics? What can the past teach
us about these mysteries? What signified the one
that came in 1929? What is the prospect for another in the approaching future?

But when we attempt to begin our studies of loan
expansions, money troubles, and the entire list of
conventional economic bugbears, let us be careful not
to "confuse effects with cause, and mistake what is
subordinate or incidental, for the principal fact."

Our good friend, Senator Burton warned against
that, and he was rather an old hand at this business.[1]

It is the purpose of this work to undertake a journey into a region as yet unexplored—into that complex, human problem of a century of Wall Street's
panics; and if, in our travels, we should chance to
light upon some discovery that may correct the great
and useful machinery of the Street, in its function of
raising capital for business by selling its paper and
marketing it upon our fifteen millions of newly-
created investors, we shall accomplish a step forward
in curbing waste, destruction, losses—and regrets.

[1] Theodore E. Burton: *Financial Crises and Periods of Industrial and Commercial Depression.*

5

I

THE GREAT INFLATION

I

ON THE UP-AND-UP

ONE of those glorious but illusive afternoons
of the summer of 1929, with Old Trinity and
the gloomy Sub-Treasury lying huddled within
shadows of steel-framed masonry,—those step-pyra-
mids of banking corporations piled up in the last few
years of the Great Inflation.

Pouring through Nassau, Broad and Wall Streets,
crowding narrow sidewalks in the majesty of numbers, to the "shuff-shuff" of countless footfalls: bank
runners, put-'n'-call men, commission house messengers, bill brokers, bond salesmen and the personnel
of money corporations.

Buzzing streets busied with stirring murmurs. A
crop of financial philosophers, professors of economics sounding the call of the New Era. An age
of mergers, of inventions, of science applied to industry. Innovations. Revolutionary ideas, such as
the public's flight from bonds to stocks. Common
shares had risen to a permanently higher plateau;
they would never recede; they would keep on rising.

The price index men were proving these New Era

9

arguments by their figures; tape readers and chart men supported the theories with their tables.

In a banking parlor, furnished lavishly, though with apparent simplicity, in cubist chairs and a modernist setting, a group of gentlemen had gathered, in high confidence, about their mahogany conference table. Financiers of that type which reaches its highest perfection in Wall Street. Fastidiously tailored. They displayed firmly chiseled features. They were undoubtedly possessed of a business judgment that was not prone to error. They were listening seriously to the words of a client who stood before them.

The speaker was cast in a different mold. He was talking of big transactions. He was a promoter who, in twenty years, had jumped from nothing to the ownership of a three-hundred-million-dollar corporation. It was operating, we will say, wire-screen plants all over the world. For, as it is now fashionable for the novelists to announce, all the characters in the accompanying episodes are imaginary, and not portraits of any living person. They are intended merely to present a composite picture of this time and period.

So this orator, blackhaired, blackeyed, with a trace of vanity displayed on his smiling lips, described his ambitious set-up, with vehement gestures. He reminded his bankers that this was an age of mergers, predicated upon higher earnings through lower production costs. So he had bought up the stocks of his chief competitors with a blunt disregard for values. Borrowing money on this collateral, he had gathered in more shares; now he practically controlled the wire-screen industry of the universe.

The promoter related that he was now nursing an immense proposition. He asked the coöperation of the bankers in launching on the stock market a heavy bond issue, with warrants convertible into millions of shares of new stock. This financial achievement would consolidate his properties into a holding company, giving him monopoly of the wire-screen business.

The financiers grouped about the board table conceded that the wire-screen man was a crude genius. Vain and willful he might be, but his promotions had been profitable to them. Their faith in the man had been of a practical nature,—they and their moneyed friends had advanced him nearly one hundred million dollars; and that was pretty steep credit with which to favor one man.

In the seclusion of the banking parlor, the great merger was carefully discussed. The bankers had financed many similar projects in the last few months, one on top of the other, and with unvarying success.

But, as they explained to the promoter, the underwriter assumes heavy responsibilities. They were inclined to favor his proposal, but their terms would be pretty severe; they would have to charge him a commission of ten per cent on the underwriting; they must also receive a bonus of quarter of a million shares of the new stock.

There was every prospect for expecting success for the flotation. The new era had created millions of new-fledged investors, and while their demands lasted, there would be no end to good times in Wall Street. Besides, the new school economists had planted in the public mind the lesson of the flight from bonds to stocks—the splendid theory that common shares promised higher profits and surer incomes than bonds. And so a fat stock bonus to the bankers would interest the latter in advancing the quotations on 'Change.

While leaving these ambitious contrivers, for a while, to develop their plans for making innumerable wire-screens and countless dollars, it may be well to turn attention to another invention made during the Great Inflation. This was the "split-up." When, under the impetus of greedy buying, the stock of a company advanced to $200 or $300 a share, the ordinary investor regarded it as too high for his purse. Then wise directors split-up such securities, say at

five-for-one, or even ten-for-one. Thus they reduced the price of the scrip to the more tempting
figure of $20 or $30. A harmless deception, for the
real value of the stock remained the same.

In Wall Street was a financier whose executive
offices controlled hundreds of companies engaged in
the manufacture of famous breakfast-foods. Their
plants skylined the expanse of thirty to forty States.
Than he, there was no abler master of the art of the
"split-up." The financial intricacies of his corporation perplexed even the keenest accountants. The
nature and variety of his security issues, major and
minor, prior and junior, underlying, pledged, cumulative preferred and prior preferred, dizzied the
imagination. The popularity of his $100 par value
stock was so great, that its quoted figures reached
exalted proportions.

This financier radiated personality; he was eagerly
hearkened to at public meetings; he was a wise judge
of the mentality of the middle classes; he raised the
bulk of his capital from modest investors whose
collective savings assume such an enormous total; so
he placed his stock in easier reach of them, by split-
ting up the $100 shares into five-for-one. Thus he
reduced their face value to $20 each. Under the
impetus of the new era teachings, even these reduced
shares gained a market value beyond the reach of

slender purses. So the clever financier split-up his $20 shares into four-for-one. Thus he created an imperial issue of thirty million shares at $5 face value.

This gifted company manager combined, with his great stores of energy, an imagination worthy that of the Barber's Brother with his Tray of Glassware. He paid dividends of six per cent in stock and six per cent in cash. But the cash dividend was calculated on the $5 face value. It meant a distribution to shareholders of only a few cents a year. Now the stock dividend— Ah, a far different matter! The higher the shares were pushed in the market, the higher in value became the stock dividend. In other words, our financier, without straining his own net earnings in the least, had invented a system *by which the stock market itself paid his investors their incomes.* Every five point advance paid one per cent more in returns to the shareholders.

There began one of the most efficient campaigns ever attempted by private enterprise for distributing common stock. Through talks over the radio, through brokers, circulars, pamphlets, advertisements, in two score States, was broadcast the allurement of investment opportunity. Super-stock-salesmen spread the legend to small folk. If you had invested $1,000 twenty years ago, you'd have $40,-000 to-day. Provide for the family's future! Get together the fund for sending your kiddies to college!

Hundreds of thousands were thus persuaded. The common stock advanced in price to $70, representing an outstanding market value of two billion dollars. The horn of plenty, fashioned by "split-ups," fairly threatened to overflow.

Also, the benefits of chain units had been discovered: chains of cigar stores, chains of moving picture houses, chains of grocery stores. The theory was now applied to chains of banks.

Putting one's money in railroads or industrials— that's often a speculative adventure. Rich men put their money in bank stocks. The president of a great Wall Street bank, member of the Federal Reserve System, considered that the time had come for the little fellows to invest in bank stocks also.

Twelve years before, this banker owned only one bank. Its resources were four million dollars. Then he began buying up other banks and their branches. In five years, he had five branch banks and fifty millions in resources. He kept on buying banks. In three more years, he had ten branches and one hundred and ten millions in resources. Still he kept on buying other banks, paying constantly higher prices for their stocks. In another year he had sixty branch banks, and $350,000,000 in resources.

In his resplendent counting-rooms were posted

framed maxims to encourage depositors: THRIFT IS
THE KEYNOTE OF SUCCESS! LET THIS BANK BE YOUR
FRIEND!

In his inner office, the banker developed his plan
for enriching the little fellows, *i.e.*, his depositors.
He had four hundred thousand depositors. He dic-
tated a letter to them. He showed that if they had
bought ten shares of his bank stock twelve years ago,
and had subsequently exercised all subscription rights
and privileges, they would have made a profit of
$50,000. He now offered each stockholder the right
to subscribe to ten shares of his stock at $200 a share
—a total investment of $2,000; and while he did not
state outright that a similar profit would be made, in
comparison with former years, nevertheless the
intimation of his letter was inescapable: each investor
would find himself proportionally enriched by similarly fat profits in time to come.

The astute banker calculated that if only ten per
cent of his depositors accepted his offer—say 40,000
—he would sell 400,000 shares of stock. In other
words, $80,000,000 in deposits now lying in his banks
to the credit of depositors would thus be transferred
to his own bank capital. A fine stroke of business for
himself, his bank, his group of stockholders, as well
as for the little fellows who would become investors
in gilt-edged securities known as bank stocks.

16

Yonder, by craning one's neck, could be glimpsed the twelfth floor windows of a skyscraper,—those of an influential brokerage house, engaged in major manipulations. Six or seven gentlemen reclining in deep comfortable chairs. News, bond and stock tickers clattered away. On the wall, the translux pictured the moving tape quotations.

Witness the members of a "stock pool." Manipulating stock of a company manufacturing a motor car accessory—a novel, cost-saving invention. Inventions, said the professors, possessed a high cash value, —a lesson which this pool was demonstrating in the stock market.

The pool was not confining itself only to the art of boosting quotations. It also distributed information. Printed in money paragraphs, slipped into news service sheets, wired to distant brokerage houses, telegraphed to branch offices, circulated in confidential whispers by customers' men: *A contract had been signed by Henry Ford for the use of this invention on his millions of motor cars!* So, at odd moments, on these summer days, the stock of the motor accessory shot up suddenly ten or twelve points, and only the chuckling "insiders" knew the reason why.

Revolutionary inventions! Profits from science! The more recent the invention, the higher the ratio of prices to earnings. Promising innovations. Motion and sound pictures and radios. Especial emphasis laid on the profits that were to come from the air in the new aeronautical stocks, shares in aircraft, airport, air transport, air line companies.

An army of men from the West had arrived in the Street. Having access to Wall Street's machinery, they used it to create imaginary values on a scale never dreamed of before. Giants of a new breed, they were greater than the Vanderbilts, the Harrimans and the Morgans of the past.[1] They seized hold of Anaconda, General Motors, Cast Iron Pipe, International Nickel, Radio, International Harvester, and drove up their shares from five to six hundred per cent. They boasted that they *had made the market*, that they were the largest individual winners, and eventually they celebrated their success at a famous dinner at the Biltmore.[2]

There was also a genius of promotions who had founded a concern to make low-priced cars, in the hope of winning success and harvesting profits rivaling those of Henry Ford. He sold fifty to sixty million dollars' worth of stock to more than 140,000 enchanted shareholders.

Still another epoch-making discovery had been achieved by the financial philosophers: investment

[1] Earl Sparling: *Mystery Men of Wall Street.*
[2] *New York Times*, April 20, 1928, p. 25.

trusts! The professors had lighted upon a "startling corollary." It was this: "If we can, by sufficient diversification in investments, get a greater certainty, and thus run less risks from our speculation, then the more unsafe investments are, taken individually, the safer they are collectively." Thus a man would make more money in such risky investments, than if he had placed his savings and earnings in sound securities.

Financiers bought railway common stocks for the purpose of controlling such roads. They loaned the collateral to bankers and bought more stocks. But when call money jumped to twenty per cent, the carrying of these loads became oppressive to the financiers, and hazardous to the bankers. Then these gentlemen invented the railroad "holding company." All the stocks were pooled; deposited in the safety vaults of the trustees. Against the pooled paper were issued collateral trust bonds, cumulative preferred and common stocks. The public fell over itself in snapping up the holding company stocks. Why not? They were issued by the biggest banking houses in the Street.

But one could continue indefinitely to recapitulate the underwritings, promotions, speculations that seethed and boiled in those delirious summer days. That brilliant radio merger. Wonderful potentialities that made a farm implement company's stock jump sky-high. The railway group whose Utopian minds planned a huge issue of the road's common shares in order to pay with the proceeds the back dividends on the preferred.

It is Wall Street's credo to stay sanguine. Its greatest banker coined the proverb that no man can expect to make money by selling his country short. Besides, being an optimist is an act of patriotism.

In the flight from bonds to common stocks, the latter reached their higher level,—the plateau from which they would never recede. Those who bought, merely paid present sums for an infinite series of future incomes. So asserted the financial philosophers; the chart-men and the price-index-men substantiated them; tape-readers, their eyes on the translux, divined that share values would advance indefinitely—indefinitely. . . .

No mere random rumors, these. They came from the lips of authority, from solid financiers, from teachers of the new political economy. High pressure salesmen traveled the country, spreading the doctrine. Motion picture audiences were educated through the movietone. In millions of suburban homes, on summer evenings, while the radio buzzed, earnest talkers over the microphone exhorted their listeners to invest the family savings in common stocks, as a safeguard against life's hazards, as an earnest of future competence!

The great machine of Wall Street had set all this in motion.

Yes, Wall Street, itself, guaranteed the integrity of the Great Inflation. Even when money rates rose under the strain. Even when the Federal Reserve Board tried to shut off stock market credit. On that day sounded a voice from the National City Bank, whose lofty and massive colonnade, with fluted Ionic columns, shadows forth the great work of Isaiah Rogers. From that deeply recessed portico, came the voice of its Chairman, offering the brokers multi-millions for the furtherance of speculation.

The furious heart of Wall Street pulsated on the Stock Exchange,—that home of an ancient brotherhood. From the open windows on its trading floor came a subdued roaring, made up of the cries of brokers congested within about the trading posts—five million share days—ten million share days—twelve million share days—a day to come of sixteen million shares.

But across the way, in that white building, whose windows open discreetly upon an inner court, heavier and heavier were the underwritings, executed without intermittence, in the secrecy and silence of its banking parlors.

II

AND now an abrupt change in Wall Street's atmosphere. The genial warmth of summer surrendered to the chill of autumn. Few in the present generation will soon forget those smashing days of October and November, when the broadest stock market of history met its most amazing fall.

From Broadway to William, from Cedar Street to beyond Exchange Place, men in customers' rooms, staring into inverted glass bowls, or glaring at the translux on the walls, across which glided the quotations. And such quotations! Shares which had sold for $300, for $500, for $700, and since split-up, now sliding down to $70. The terrifying surrender of once impregnable bull cliques. The throwing over of ballast by the ringleaders of the consortium,— they, who had sworn assurances of an endless rise.

Once more we find ourselves in that banking parlor, with its futuristic setting, where the great wire-screen merger had been developed. Here, also, there was a distinct change in the atmosphere. The promoter, the self-willed, blackhaired genius of combinations, had just arrived. He had been hurriedly summoned by his bankers.

How changed, those financiers again grouped about the mahogany table; those fairweather friends, who had once listened to his plans so pleasantly; who had favored him with friendly words and the substantial backing from their money vaults! They now welcomed him with hard eyes and frozen faces.

The big merger, raised upon the expectation of higher earnings through low production costs, was, lamentable to relate, suddenly facing financial disaster. The underwriting plan which was to consolidate the properties into a holding company,—the convertible bonds and the millions of common stock, all had been ready for launching, when the crash had come.

Yes, those bankers, so infallible, so experienced, so wise, had made a miscalculation. In Wall Street, as in other spheres of life, men do not readily admit their errors.

The chairman of the banking group addressed their client in a tone of severity. His words seemed to sense a suspicion that the other was trying to welsh on his obligations by refusing to meet his creditors. Yes, the financiers were no longer his financial accomplices; they were his creditors; and this was no time for evasions.

23

Did the promoter realize his true position? So asked the chairman of the money-lenders. Was he not aware that those stocks which he had bought so recklessly to effect his merger, had now dropped nearly a hundred dollars a share? And he had borrowed money on those stocks. The collateral had now shrunk to a mere fifth of its former value.

In fact, not to split hairs any longer, they had summoned him here to make good. They were going to call his loans.

Their client contented himself with an expressive gesture, which seemed to include the whole of Wall Street, through which thoroughfare one could sense the crowds rushing past, with fear-implanted faces. Why blame him for conditions? He wasn't the only one in a fix. Besides, they were in it as deep as he. Hadn't they promised to finance him?

In cutting tones, the presiding banker informed his creditor that no group of underwriters would be insane enough to attempt to sell securities in such a market. Bonds and stocks were unsalable. "Besides," he added, "there are quite thirty banks, not only in Wall Street, but in most of the seaboard cities, who are demanding that you meet your loans. To-morrow, perhaps, there will be millions in judgments against your companies. *Do you realize that you owe one hundred million dollars?*"

The promoter now faced his tormenter. He demanded irritably: "And how should I raise a hundred millions?"

"Then you admit you're bankrupt!" triumphantly exclaimed the chairman.

Although the principals in this secluded drama might not have been conscious of it for the moment, yet this scene had had a classic precedent. Twenty-two years before, in the floodtide of the panic of 1907, another such situation had arisen. Then the greatest merchant in the United States had been called to his bankers' offices in Wall Street. They had refused him an extension of his loans. And that eminent master of the yard-stick had protested indignantly that their demands, however reasonable in normal times, were at that moment unwarranted.

"Then you admit your bankruptcy!" the scornful bankers had exclaimed.

But the great merchant had drawn himself up proudly. He had uttered the historic phrase: "I'm too big a man for you to let me fail!"

He was right. He owed too much to be abandoned. This debtor's ruin would have bankrupted the drygoods merchants of the country. The bankers did not let him fail. They "trusteed" him.

Now, on a day in '29, nearly a quarter of a century later, when great financiers flung at their borrower the terrifying sentence: "You are bankrupt!" their debtor recovered his equipoise. He knew he owed too much to be thrown overboard. He smiled in the faces of his onetime friends. "If you're going to break me, well then,—*I'll see you going into the screen business!*"

Alas, it was true. The bankers dared not precipitate his company into receivership. And they "trusteed" him,—in other words, they took over his screen business.

In Wall Street, as elsewhere, things are not always what they seem. The Street is a machine for money-making. But its capital is not its own. The promoter does not back his schemes with his own bankroll. He manufactures stocks and bonds. But his bankers do not loan their own money upon these securities; they "underwrite" them for profit. They intend to pass them on into the hands of that unknown quantity—the public. But when the public's funds take flight, financing fails, underwritings are abandoned.

This was by no means an isolated circumstance in those eventful days when values went next to nothing; when brokers closed the Exchange, because free trading meant ruin; when the bourses of the world shuddered under the weight of liquidation; when, like the continuous rattle of musketry, sounded reports of small bank failures. These latter were due to embezzlements of funds squandered by officers in stock speculation.

For instance, how had the great master of "split-ups" fared in his soaring plans? That gifted financier, the Barber's Brother, the dispenser of breakfast-foods? He had promised to enrich his stockholders, not by tapping his net profits—but by the amazing argument that with every five points' advance, his shareholders gained another dollar in income. On the very first day of the October crash, it was his stock on which the crisis centered. Six million shares were flung wildly upon the market. In four or five days, the astounding issue sank to only a fraction of its former quotations. The drop consumed ten times five points. All that glorious paper income had fizzled out. The corporation, itself, was sound and prosperous. There was no doubt about that. But its common capitalization, which had been tossed up to a value of two billions, had shrunk to half a billion in less than a week.

Simple-minded souls, persuaded by the glib tongues of radio broadcasters, saw the provision for their families' future go glimmering. Induced by high-pressure salesmen to buy shares on installments, they were faced with contracts compelling them to pay three times more for a commodity than it was now worth. Many lost investments, the money for which had been drawn from their savings banks.

Those disillusioned shareholders were victims of the reverse action of a brilliant theory. They had learned a lesson not embraced in the teachings of the new economic school: *the permanence of one's capital is of more importance than profits based on market advances.* That is an ancient rule as immutable as the mountains.

Losses had come not only to investors in mergers and split-ups. Bank stocks had dropped in single days from one to five hundred dollars a share, cutting down fortunes of the wealthiest men. The president of the chain banks, which were members of the Federal Reserve System, who had framed his maxims: THRIFT IS THE KEYNOTE OF SUCCESS! and LET THIS BANK BE YOUR FRIEND!, had been plunged into an embarrassing position. He had induced the "little fellows," depositors in his sixty branches, no doubt with the best intentions in the world, to invest in his inflated shares. But only three months after his signed, circular letter had gone out, the stock of his bank had sunk to only one-third of its former value.

This sanguine banker's depositors saw their balances shrink to the tune of some sixty-four million dollars. They had paid $2,000 for ten shares of stock on the recommendation of the man to whom they had entrusted their money. These shares were now worth not much more than $400 in the over-the-counter market. Even after the passage of a year they went still lower, for the bank cut its dividend. So much for the integrity of the new philosophy. So much for discounting future dividends and earnings by paying inflated prices for chain stocks.

Meanwhile that decorative room on the twelfth floor of the Wall Street skyscraper was at present unoccupied by the members of the exclusive "gentlemen's pool." The stock of their motor car accessory, after having been manipulated to an amazing figure by the prevarications of the pool's tipsters, had been overtaken by successive crashes, until it was now selling for only a few dollars a share.

That subtly whispered "Ford contract" had been a myth. Through the medium of the New York Stock Exchange's machinery, the pool had unloaded on their dupes in splendid fashion. With their bank balances fattened, its members had now gone into retirement. No more tips were being handed out. The news paragraphs had ceased appearing. Dejected customers' men had no explanations available for their indignant clients.

29

The silence of the grave had descended upon this market adventure. The principals were mum. They feared, perhaps, they might be liable to prosecution under Section 926 of the Penal Law.

But the pool had demonstrated the falsity of the theory of the professors that, since science and invention had become handmaids to industry, shares issued on inventions must necessarily possess a high cash value.

All those enterprises exploited on the glamor of Henry Ford's success,—those Fordized industries— had been sucked down into the "air-pockets" of the market's collapse. Many of that invading army of "Western giants" had motored to Florida to lick their wounds in silence. The talented promoter, who, it may be remembered, had set out to emulate the King of Dearborn, by manufacturing flivvers, had sold millions of shares of common stock, raising many more millions of dollars. Sad to relate, he had never earned a penny for his stockholders. Indeed, many had practically lost their investments. The shares had sunk to less than two dollars apiece.

And that brilliant radio merger—it had dropped into bankruptcy after its sponsors admitted that they had sold out on the public. But of all the fortune-promising innovations, the airplane ventures had won the booby prize; most of these aeronautical, aircraft

30

and air line stocks had nose-dived into oblivion; their shares were no longer quoted; there were no prices to quote.

And the investment trusts! Those epoch-making discoveries, in which, if one put his savings and earnings, he could make more money on the riskiest propositions than if he invested in gilt-edge securities! How had this remarkable theory stood the test? Truth to tell, the investment trusts had made a ghastly showing. They had sold bonds, cumulative preferred, A, B, and C shares, and common stocks. They had put the money into overvalued securities. In the Great Deflation, their assets slumped with it.·

One of these precious organizations, affiliated with a dozen smaller trusts, in the drear days of autumn, had collapsed, with its allied companies. It seemed that they had merely bought and sold one another's shares. Not a dollar in money had passed among them. Prosecution faced their officers. Indeed, many of the trusts were restrained, enjoined, accused of fraud by the State Bureau of Securities. In the better managed trusts, shareholders had fared badly; dividends paid out were only one-third of the amounts they would have received had they bought their own shares outright. Great New York Stock Exchange houses failed, and the investment trusts they had sponsored were exposed as examples of dishonest management.

The railroad holding companies had proved a similar disappointment. The bankers had received back the loans they had made to the financiers. The latter still controlled the railroads through the collateral of the holding companies. The public carried the bag,—*i.e.*, it had put its money into the common stocks, which had dropped to a fraction of their former value. And, for the greater number, no dividends were in prospect.

"On the stock market itself, there is little need for moralizing," wrote the experienced financial editor of the *New York Times*, on October 30, 1929, even before the worst aspect of the panic had spent itself. "It has told its own story and taught its own lesson. . . . Of the extraordinary illusions concerning finance, economics and Prosperity, which for two years past have been defended and encouraged by men whose position gave small excuse for such an attitude, it is not necessary now to speak. These intellectual vagaries, too, have gone down in the Wall Street storm."

The great Wall Street captains had prophesied that a nation of investors, with unlimited purses, would continue buying stocks indefinitely. But it was now evident that that nation's surplus capital had been eaten up. It had been sported with, siphoned into the unknown. The capitalist was involved, the manufacturer, the merchant, the shopkeeper, the butcher, the baker, the candlestickmaker —nobody's resources had been overlooked.

The foregoing episodes, grouped together, are instructive. They show us how the most practical-minded people in the world raise the capital necessary for their industries. It is a prodigal and thriftless method.

We have just witnessed the source of the country's greatest economic waste.

Much harm had been done by broadcasting the lesson that "the common stock absorbs the advantage which bonds, because of their fixed return, in dollars, cannot absorb. The common stock will go up to the extent that the bonds and preferred stocks cannot go up."[1]

Teachers of the new philosophy had not foreseen that, *per contra*, common stocks will also go down to the extent that bonds and preferred stocks cannot go down.

What had the financial philosophers to say? "The slump in stock prices," said one of them, "destroyed no physical assets. As stock prices gradually rose

[1] *The Stock Market Crash—And After:* Irving Fisher, Professor of Economics, Yale University, 1930, p. 261.

33

from the panic bottom, it was found that, to a very large extent, the crash in prices had robbed thousands of Peters to pay a very few Pauls." [2]

Rather unfeeling, that, to a world bamboozled, a nation gulled, a people cleverly plundered of their savings; to the unsuspecting family, deluded in its home nest by persuasive salesmanship and insidious radio broadcasting; to small folk, thus impoverished, who, in the three months of the ending year, were compelled to draw hundreds of millions from savings banks in New York City; to war veterans who, in a single week, made loan applications for fifteen millions; to holders of life insurance, who in one November week borrowed a total of twenty millions on security of their policies; to uncertain millions of unemployed, roaming the streets.

Over all such visible reactions lay a sinister inference: they represented losses in stock buying; they were drafts on accumulated reserves, which had undermined the savings of a country's thrifty class.

Then ensued a remarkable dénouement, a repetition of scenes now "old in story." Bankers, heads of corporations, industrial leaders, cried their dismay. Some one was certainly to blame for the catastrophe. A financier placed the fault upon Congress; it had

[2] *The Stock Market Crash—And After:* Irving Fisher, Professor of Economics, Yale University, 1930, p. 261.

34

delayed tariff legislation. A financial professor blamed inflationary banking. Bull operators denounced their enemies, the bear cliques. And comedy o'ertopped the tragedy, when a high stock operator—whose own company promotions have been a source of loss and chagrin to his shareholders—reproached the President.[3] The Federal Reserve Board, he said, had precipitated the panic.[4] And all these deductions and conclusions were distinguished by the usual contradictions, inconsistencies and disagreements.

That was an amazing fact! Why, these were the most practical minds that our civilization has produced,—the men of Wall Street, who had loaned out the public's millions; the chairmen of ancient corporations, who, in emitting capital issues, had placed no end to their borrowings; the promoters who had pyramided their projects, the syndicate operators who had churned up prices.

A stormy day had arrived in October; its breath had disturbed Wall Street's confidence; it had shown its atmosphere of authority and assurance to be a delusion; what had been thought impossible had come about; and the Street admitted that it could not understand.

[3] Earl Sparling: *Mystery Men of Wall Street.*
[4] *Commercial and Financial Chronicle,* Jan.-March, 1928, p. 286: "The Reserve Banks, by their policy, aided Stock Exchange speculation indirectly, but they never do it directly."

35

Was the financial downfall of 1929 then some phenomenon, an event without precedent, a cataclysm beyond parallel?

Why, not at all. Panics are as old as Wall Street. Their stageplay has prevailed for one hundred years. These psychical phenomena were familiar to the Street far back in the "brave days of old," when the weather-beaten Sub-Treasury was still a virgin white Doric temple; even before Isaiah Rogers built his Merchants' Exchange, and raised the lofty colonnade which lives to-day in the portico of the National City Bank.

And yet, for the time being, the Street had forgotten its own past; forgotten the currency embroilments of '37; the wild October 13th, twenty years after, with its mobs a-riot; the hysterias of September, '73; the wrack of the great adventurers of '84; the terrors of '93, when all the fat of the monopolies was in the fire; the railroad exasperations of 1901; the black year of 1907, when the very devil was to pay with coppers and the banks.

To the Street, the panic, as an abstract thing, constitutes the great enigma; it still is the least understood of any event that rules its life.

Fortified with fresher knowledge, a newer experience, a clearer viewpoint, is it possible for our generation to find a preventive for the panic? It is a

36

difficult and complex undertaking. Perhaps, before seeking a remedy, it may be found wise to make a study of the thing itself. What is the panic? An answer to this question would be a triumph of discovery. Possibly it may be found in the records of the Street, and with the useful purpose in mind, it is the object of this book to pilot the reader through the obscure byways of that adventure.

III

INQUIRY INTO THE PANIC

IT might be an act of wisdom on our part not to rely too absolutely upon the well-known aspects of the panic. It would be unfortunate were we to expend our efforts upon a study of its effects, while ignoring its cause. We should, perhaps, take a longer view by first propounding the question, "What is a panic?" before undertaking the solution of, "Why did it come about?"

The word, of course, is as old as the thing itself.

Pan, the bogie god, frightening lonely rustics in the land of the vine and olive; psychological fright, —unreasoning fear, communicated in the mob.

Now one will find that no other subject has so puzzled the heads of the financial philosophers. But in general, they have agreed that it places *finis* to a period to which the name of "cycle" has been given.

The classic conception of the cycle begins always with a display of wonderful prosperity; with a jump in the birth rate of new enterprises, of inventions, land booms, real estate speculations, company

38

mergers; with a rise in salaries, rentals, wages of workingmen; with corporations raiding the stock market for fresh capital; with speculative syndicates and pool operators shooting up quotations; with bond salesmen traveling from Wall Street to sell their persuasions to small capitalists and country bankers. Stock hucksters then commence ringing up "prospects" on the long distance, and customers' men begin whispering into the ears of credulous margin traders. Siren voices of speculation sound over the radio and from the movietone, while everybody is hungering for wealth and luxury. Bankers are very accommodating in encouraging loans and recommending securities. Fine fellows, those bankers, when times are so good.

One day, a check to these piping times. There is a sudden jolt, an awakening; everybody is living beyond his means, consuming other people's labor; savings are gone; all the new capital has vanished, nobody knows where, and those once genial bankers harshly call their loans. Defaults, bankruptcies, receiverships. Families beggared. That vague thing, the stock market, has swallowed huge sums stolen by desperate men. Cashiers confess, bank tellers sprint to reach the borders and men who have looted corporation treasuries crash in head-on collisions,

39

jump from airplanes and drop from seventeen-story windows.

The end of the cycle, this, and now panic comes. The great dream over, the illusion of riches has betrayed its promise, and ruin takes its place.

But, astonishing fact! After a time, the cycle's orbit is again renewed. New generations make the same gallant efforts, with fresh beginnings, endlessly repeated, but always with similar endings.

"Men obey a nameless lord of the wheel that incessantly turns on itself, and crushes the wills that have set it in motion."

All this, indeed, is very perplexing, disconcerting, mystifying, and one asks himself whether any one has ever succeeded in explaining these catastrophes. Do we really know anything, have we ever learned anything about them?

Through long custom, and by general consent, the solution to this enigma has been left to one certain group of gentlemen. They have thoroughly investigated the production, the distribution and the consumption of wealth. They have been at this work for a very long time,—far back indeed; one might venture to say so far back as 150 years. They have, during that period, emitted billions of phonological utterances, written millions upon millions of words, books of voluminous size, with terrifying titles. By this time they surely should have succeeded in elucidating their problem. But have they done so? Let us see.

From the days of Adam Smith, what haven't our distinguished economists divulged, forecast, discovered! There was Wirth, and Juglar, and John Mills, with his psychology of fluctuations; Werner Sombart, with his dissimilarity in rhythm of production; Pigou, with his waves of elation and depression, and Tugan-Baranovski, with his scarcity of capital.

But invariably, the economist finds that his predecessor has actually discovered only half-truths, and one despairs of finding any theory which alike accounts for all phenomena. The perplexed philosophers begin to be convinced that panics must be abnormal events, abstract happenings, products, perhaps, of epochal inventions, of tariff revisions or of monetary changes. Some see the origin of the catastrophe in a state of the human mind, undermining business confidence; [1] some see it in complexities of business organization, some in overtrading or in overproduction. And so they continue: Alvin Hansen, Thorstein Veblen, Professor Seligman, with his

[1] Dr. E. M. Patterson, Wharton School of Finance and Commerce, University of Pennsylvania.

blame on over-capitalized values in modern economic life.[2]

Indeed, we find that at last earthly explanations fail the learned professors of economy, for they adopt extra-terrestrial hypotheses. Jevons appears, with his theory of sunspots that influence weather, the latter influencing crops, and crops regulating cycles. And if sunspots fail to account for the phenomena, then perhaps Professor Moore's theory that the eight-yearly interposition of Venus between the Sun and the Earth may be responsible for the eight-year generating cycle.[3]

So these studious gentlemen never seem to agree.

With the new era, a change came upon the economists. Spurning their former deductions, they substituted the inductive and experimental method with realistic analyses, charts, averages, index numbers. The science of economic statistics was born.

The new economists put on tremendous pressure. One of them produced a huge volume of charts and tables dense with figures. Considering his work obsolete, he began all over again, with more elaborate charts, his tables still denser, more profound the

[2] Prof. Edwin R. A. Seligman: *The Crisis of 1907 in the Light of History,* *1907-08.*
[3] *Generating Economic Cycles:* Henry Ludwell Moore, professor of political economy, Columbia University, 1923.

quantitative and qualitative analyses, drawn not from one country, but from all countries, not for one year, but for every month in every year.

Now, buried shoulder deep in his statistical mountain, the burrowing investigator's goal is still more distant. A vast scheme! "No group of workers in the present generation can hope to cover the field."

These later economists were responsible for the new financial philosophy. We listened to their teachings during the Great Inflation, and we have just witnessed the lamentable results since the autumn of '29. Under these gentlemen, we certainly fared worse than with the old deductive school.

To-day, we are at the end of a century's investigations,—and meet only frustration. Our economists despair of explaining their phenomenon. They are not to be blamed, because their irreconcilable differences concern an intricate problem.[4] Still, it must be admitted that they have failed, and the proof lies in that they have provided no answer to the enigma of the panic; *for that answer must disclose some vital feature that is common to them all.*

It would appear that, in the first place, it was an injustice to the economists, to depend upon them for the answer. Few of them have opportunities to familiarize themselves with the Street, for a study

[4] Burton: *Financial Crises.*

of its purely human activities. In observing the events that preceded the panic of 1929, one is not impressed by the influence of economic causes. All the indexes, averages and charts of the new economists failed in giving an indication of the coming storm.

For certainly, the bankers who, at the maddest period of the Great Inflation, loaned one hundred millions toward the wire-screen merger, were interested in but a single purpose: the making of money. What other object had the genius of "split-ups," in raising his capital at the moment when the market was toppling, in violation of all financial strategy? What object, other than this, had the banking member of the Federal Reserve System in selling stock to his depositors? What other object had the pool that operated in the motor accessory, the investment trust managers who juggled the shares of their twelve companies, those syndicates that underwrote vast issues at a dangerous moment, in the hope of profiting from a public craze, and those gentlemen who celebrated their success at the Hotel Biltmore dinner?

Apparently the cataclysm was produced by blindness to economic consequences; but decidedly not by crop failure, or problems of circulation, of overproduction, of complexities of business life,—or sunspots.

44

Mr. Simmons, the former President of the Stock Exchange, publicly praised the new school of financial philosophers. He asserted that its professors were giving business a sense of direction, motive and aim which it never before possessed. And no fault can be found with his attitude. The new philosophy, in encouraging the flight from bonds to stocks, did its part in accelerating transactions on the Exchange.

In the end the public was the loser,—but business is business. It is unreasonable to expect that that of Wall Street should differ from any other. The efforts of the pool manager, the market operator, the underwriter, are directed toward making a profit. The highest banker in the Street reluctantly faces the chairman of his finance committee if he has failed to show a surplus by the end of the fiscal year.

There are no moral laws applicable here. We are dealing with the most practical factors of life. For in the last analysis of Wall Street's business, questions of ethics do not enter. Not at all. Behind illusions of phrases, dignities of imposing names, solemnities of corporate power, lie, as elsewhere, the bald facts of life.

The Street's business is to sell paper for money— to sell it at the highest price, even though it be possible that values may fall heavily. One must admit that this is the manner in which a great part of capital is raised, notwithstanding many notable exceptions.

This is the practice of Wall Street. Perhaps it should be amended, but it never has been—not in all the long years of its existence.

There is more than mere jest—rather profound insight—in the observation of old Sir Roger Orton: "Some men has plenty money and no brains; and some has plenty brains and no money;—surely, them as has plenty money and no brains, was made for them as has plenty brains and no money!"

Which brings us back to a contemplation of our recent catastrophe. It may be that one will find that the call money rates, the expansions in brokers' loans, the avalanche of security issues, were merely results and not the causes of the convulsion of 1929. It is possible that if we study the stageplay of the Street for the last century, we may find that we are contemplating only the acts of men, and that all the land speculations, the banking crises, the money movements, were merely consequences of their acts.

In other words, the panic may not be an economic development at all, but a human event.

Economic reasons, at least, have failed entirely to explain the phenomena of panics. So it may prove wise for us to let our eyes draw near, to witness this phenomenon in action; to breathe the breath of the panic; to follow its unerring progress; to watch its

46

human struggles; to study the thing itself. Where so many abler minds have preceded us, we can scarcely hope to solve the mystery. Still, we may learn something new, something heretofore unsuspected and entirely different from what has generally been accepted.

II

THE LAND CRAZE

IV

SO we step backward a full century in history.
    Immediately we encounter a great character who, with his illusions, jockeyed Wall Street, the country, and the greater part of the world, one hundred years ago.

In a country of little more than thirteen millions, the insignificant spot known as Wall Street was still negligible as a money center. But the power represented to-day by the Morgan banking group was then embodied in an imposing financial institution, the Second Bank of the United States, located in Philadelphia, in those days the stronghold of American finance.

It was therefore in Philadelphia that a figure of distinction trod the flags of Chestnut Street, in his blue coat with brass buttons, yellow nankeen pantaloons, canary-colored gloves and glossy beaver.[1] An Adonis in looks, but a wit besides, also a diplomat, a gallant, a man-of-the-world, his popularity un-

[1] Anne Hollingsworth Wharton: *Salons Colonial and Republican.*

bounded,—one beheld Nicholas Biddle, the greatest banker in America.

During the thirties, Biddle ruled the aristocratic money world with the hand of an aristocrat. It was his theory that with wealth and influence one could accomplish the seemingly impossible. Through his personality, talents and versatility, he dazzled the men of his time. He stimulated them to imitate his financial juggleries. Grandiose fancies inflamed his mind. He condescended to consider only ventures that were vast and expansive, such as cornering the world's cotton market, financing networks of canals and widespread land speculations.

"The golden calf of Chestnut and Wall Streets," they called him. For they said that, at his approach, "the well-brushed hat of the cosy millionaire, or the business-like cap of the money broker, instinctively came down from its empty eminence, while the pliant knee could with difficulty restrain its idolatrous genuflections." [2]

This world of a hundred years ago, which was gaping with surprise at the sight of steamboats traveling the Hudson River, was far different from ours of to-day; but we shall see that its people were no whit different from ourselves.

From a background of poverty, a rough Southern

[2] *Diary of Philip Hone*, Dec. 14, 1841.

soldier had ridden into Washington as President. Origin and nature had made him champion of the mechanics of the cities, the plains farmers and the pioneers struggling on the forest's fringe.

A challenging situation. The clash soon came.

Biddle, president of the Second Bank of the United States, was the haughty leader of bankers and the moneyed class. Jackson and his followers hated and feared that citadel of tyrannical power. Indeed, Jackson was convinced that the Bank had failed in its purpose of establishing a sound currency. He made it the object of bitter attacks. The great Biddle, supported by the aristocrats of the East, championed by Whig leaders, and surrounded and encouraged by flatterers, was ripe for the quarrel.[3]

Then Jackson, in his war upon the Bank, vetoed the renewal of its charter.

However, the powerful Biddle refused to be beaten when Jackson removed the ægis of the Government from the Bank of the United States. He quickly obtained a charter for it from the State of Pennsylvania. Now the proud financier was sole master of that imposing institution. But its capital of $35,-000,000 was too large for local commercial needs. Its immense funds could not be used to advantage in

[3] Charles A. Conant: *A History of Modern Banks of Issue,* New York, 1896.

a single State. Biddle's vivid and inflated fancy then
had full play. He embarked on his vast speculations
and farflung underwritings.

The eminent example of the "golden calf of
Chestnut and Wall Streets" encouraged his admirers
and imitators. It fired the imaginations of a horde
of opportunists, who began to gamble in all sorts of
land in city and country. It has been said that the
people of the thirties were not a bit different from
ourselves. The resemblance becomes more vivid on
recalling the hallucinations of our Florida land boom.
Yes, alas, human nature and Wall Street were the
same a century ago, as they are to-day, in spite of
what the "new era" enthusiasts may say. For our
kinsfolk of the thirties sold and re-sold their lands at
advancing prices, from the pine forests of Maine, to
the live-oak hammocks of the Gulf coast; from the
"water-lots" in Jersey City and Noddle's Island, to
the cotton lands of Yazoo and the prairies of Illinois.

Those early land speculators laid out new cities in
the Western wilderness. The Government sold the
wild lands at $1.25 an acre. The speculators paid for
them in notes, issued by banks they, themselves, had
organized. The Land Office deposited the notes back
into the banks, which again loaned them to the same
speculators, who used them in buying up more land.

Now in Wall Street, the leading figures in this opportunist movement that was sweeping the country off its feet, were two brothers, J. L. and S. Josephs, enterprising Jewish boys from Richmond, Va., who had founded a banking house on a capital of $20,000. Other partners joined them, Moses Henriques and two associates from Cuba, bringing to the firm $490,-000 in specie. These bankers gained prestige by being appointed New York agents for the Rothschilds. Their transactions in sterling exchange and bill discounting became enormous.[4] Then, imitating the example of the illustrious Biddle, they plunged boldly into hazardous cotton and land speculations.

Hunger for land led to a hunger for money. Specie was fairly plentiful in seaboard cities, but beyond the Alleghanies it was often still in the form of "cut money," created from Spanish milled dollars, in guineas, doubloons and other foreign coins.[5] And so money had to be manufactured daily, not only in the notes of sound banks, but in the "Brandon Bank" kind in the South and the "Wild Cat" and "Red Dog" banks of the West. Yet rapidly and recklessly as currency was issued, the want of more increased as fast.

There were 634 banks in the country, with loans of

[4] *Stocks and Stock-Jobbing in Wall-Street*, N. Y., 1848.
[5] John Bache McMaster: *History of the People of the U. S.*, Vol. IV.

$525,000,000 and specie back of the loans of only $38,000,000; their position grew weaker daily.

Politics divided the two leading figures of the time,—Biddle and Jackson. Its animosities had also split up the banking groups of Wall Street. In the closing days of the previous century, Alexander Hamilton had organized the Bank of New York, but the Liberals or Republicans complained that the bank denied them fair treatment. So Aaron Burr, Hamilton's political opponent, had founded the Bank of the Manhattan Company. This rivalry led finally to the storied duel below the heights of Weehawken.[6] But Burr left a legacy of hatred to the bank he had founded.

President Jackson condemned the rush for public wild lands. He issued his "specie circular," demanding that payments for land should be made only in specie or notes of specie value. He prohibited the deposit of Federal revenues in the United States Bank, and distributed them amongst State banks favorable to the administration. The Bank of the Manhattan Company and the Dry Dock, being pro-Jackson, and recipients of government deposits, were denounced as "pet banks," and consequently regarded with furious hatred by the Whigs.

[6] *Iconography of Manhattan Island:* I. N. Phelps Stokes, Vol. 5, Chapter IV. *New York Evening Post*, Wed., July 19, 1804.

The weakness of the Wall Street banks was to be aggravated by hard luck. On a December night in '35, fire destroyed the Merchants' Exchange, the pride of the Street, built of Westchester marble. Its great dome fell in with a tremendous crash. Seventeen blocks of buildings were destroyed, with a real property loss of $18,000,000. Many a Wall Street man, "who had retired to his pillow in affluence, was a bankrupt on awaking."

The stock board of the brokers was destroyed in the burning of the Exchange. In the general distress, they were driven to install their new Board of Brokers in a room that had once served as a hayloft for a stable in the rear of the once stylish home of Mr. Jauncey.[7]

Immediately a furious re-building began during the wave of false prosperity. Under the patronage of the Rothschilds, the business of the Josephs brothers had swollen so that they needed a larger banking house. They began to put up a pretentious granite structure at Wall and Hanover Streets.

Fire? Destruction? No matter: all sails were set ahead by the gallant enthusiasts of the thirties, under the leadership and example of the dazzling financial adventurer, Nicholas Biddle. Flush of enormous

[7] John F. Watson: *Annals, etc. of New York, Phila.,* 1846, p. 353.

capital, Biddle was prodigal with loans. He was willing to advance his bank's money on almost any sort of enterprise. He grasped at millions and sported with them as a high banker. But he openly scorned the dull and dry details of investigating what he considered trifles. Such work, he contended, was fit occupation only for mean minds.

Land booms! Cotton gambles! The whole country had been drawn into the movement. Gamesters and fortune hunters building phantom cities. Paper banks of the South and West, churning out their notes. In Wall Street, the Josephs brothers plunging in the vanguard of a moving mass of lesser speculators, whose ventures Biddle readily underwrote. In the Street, where fire had destroyed so many real millions, the bankers were fighting one another. Their banks were tottering under heavier and heavier burdens of loans. Specie began to vanish. A great panic was approaching.

On March 14, 1837, came a peculiar happening. Walls of the gorgeous new bank building of the Josephs brothers, near Hanover Street, began to crack and settle, while it was nearing completion. The entire mass suddenly collapsed. The concussion of its fall shook the foundations of every building in the district.[8]

[8] *New York Commercial Advertiser*, March 14, 1837.

V

THE panic struck Wall Street with brutal suddenness.

There was then no telegraph to foretell its coming.

A swift packet had flown from the South on the wings of the wind. It arrived Friday, March 17, just three days after the collapse of the Josephs brothers' bank building.

Faces showed long and grave in counting-houses. Men began rushing wildly to and from coffee-houses and taverns.

The packet had brought news of commercial disaster. In the rich city of New Orleans, the greatest cotton houses in the country had gone under with staggering losses. Nearly one-fifth of the bank directors were insolvent. The city's commerce was in awful shape. Its indebtedness, in liabilities of cotton factors and land speculations, was stupendous. Close to $200,000,000!

The great land boom had crashed. The cotton corner was broken.

How would all this react upon Wall Street? The

59

answer soon came. The firm of J. L. & S. Josephs & Company stopped payment in consequence of the New Orleans failures. Credulous folk now gathered about the ruins of their new bank building. They saw in this coincidence some supernatural warning of the failure. But the collapse had been due merely to the weakness of a jerry-built structure.

Near William Street, before the entrance to the Jauncey stable, where the Board of Brokers met, there hung a white-faced crowd. Prices of stocks were falling on 'Change in a way that Wall Street had never known before.

The banks offered to accommodate the Josephs brothers with a million and a half. But the bankers pleaded that they would need a million more credit before they could resume business. Other houses went under before the night closed. All were heavy failures, both of merchants and brokers.

Fearful crisis in the money market. All minds turned at once toward Nicholas Biddle, the resourceful, the unconquerable president of the United States Bank of Pennsylvania. A deputation of Whig merchants at once traveled to Philadelphia, to appeal to the representative of their class and party.[1] The great banker was undismayed. As usual, he began to sport with his millions. He would ship a million in specie

[1] *New York Commercial Advertiser*, March 29, 1837.

to London; but the Wall Street banks must also remit a like sum. The day on which this action was taken, proved the most gloomy ever experienced in the Street. Another row of houses failed. Stocks were still on the fall. Frightened merchants hovered in the financial district until late that night.

Rumors now about the Mechanics' Bank. John Fleming, its president, had resigned. The Street was thrown into terror when it learned that Fleming had been found dead in his home. A run followed upon the bank.[2] These bank runs of '37 were different from the ones with which our day is familiar. They consisted of a frantic onrush of the poorer people, who demanded cash for the paper money which had been issued by the bank.

The catalogue of failures was swelled to 352. Silver and small change vanished through swift and secret channels. This caused widespread alarm. Much of this specie was disappearing into the "tills of chests in Dutchess and Ulster Counties—tied up in stocking-feet in Long Island and New Jersey towns."[3]

Financial convulsion engulfed the entire country. The influx of capital from Europe ceased. The whole South went bankrupt. Nine-tenths of the merchants of Mobile suspended. Tobacco shared the

[2] *Ibid.*, May 4, 1837.   [3] *Ibid.*, May 8, 1837.

61

fate of cotton. Imagined values of great possessions
in the West vanished into thin air. Fortunes in city
lots disappeared overnight. Names of paper towns
located in the wilderness sounded like ghastly jests.[4]

Nicholas Biddle's remittance of two millions in
specie to London failed to reëstablish American credit
abroad. The Whigs calculated that there were about
$80,000,000 in specie in the country, which sum was
to 13,000,000 people about six dollars apiece. Men
with assets of a million were failing for $40,000 or
less. Men with real estate enough to pay their debts
twenty times over, were failing, for specie currency
being the order of the day, credit could not be created,
even on real estate.

Wall Street Whigs sent a committee to Washington. They determined to force President Van Buren
to reverse the policy of his predecessor. They demanded a repeal of the "specie order." They denounced the substitution of a metallic for a paper
currency. Yes, Wall Street banks insisted upon the
benefits of a paper currency, even of the non-specie-
paying banks. To-day, the financial district regards
paper inflation as the deadly sin. *Tempora mutan-
tur!*

When Van Buren refused to meet their demands,
the Whigs opened floodgates of invective: " 'Perish

[4] Carl Schurz: *Henry Clay,* Boston and New York, 1887.

commerce! Perish credit! Perish the institutions of our country!' were the watch-words of Jackson-Van Burenism in 1834. Well, they have perished!"

Wall Street *versus* Washington—how old the feud! 'Twas the same old story, ever new, even though in '37 there was no Federal Reserve Board to face the denunciations of the Street's great market gamblers, as in 1929.

A despairing conviction came to Wall Street that no aid was to be expected. This intensified the quarrel of the banker-politicians. Under the leadership of the Bank of New York, the Whigs tried to crush their rivals, the Bank of the Manhattan Company and the Dry Dock Bank, the "pet banks" favored by the administration.

So another bank run soon electrified the Street. This time it was on the Dry Dock, and under the avalanche of bill-holders clamoring for specie, the bank was broken. In the terror-complex, a general run now followed on all the banks in the city.[5]

Only a fortnight before, the cash in the New York banks had amounted to $3,000,000. On the evening of May 9, this amount had shrunk to a fraction below $1,600,000. The Whig bankers decided to suspend cash payments. But three institutions, headed by the Bank of the Manhattan Company, feeling secure in

[5] *New York Commercial Advertiser*, May 8, 1837.

the friendship of the administration, opposed this action. Indeed, the Bank of the Manhattan Company refused to pay out its own notes, but distributed those of its weaker rivals.

Then the Whigs threatened to direct the storm of the panic upon the banks of the Democrats. The latter, realizing that they would soon be stripped of their cash, submitted to the will of the majority. The suspension of specie payments was decided upon.[6]

In New York there was a wide gap between the slum-dwellers, in their rags and misery, and the well-to-do, haughty of race and dominant in the control of place and property, across which was bridged no bond of sympathy. This class hatred had been shown in the great fire of '35, when misery roamed the ashes of Wall Street, searching for abandoned treasures. And, drunk from wines and liquors found in ruined stores, it mocked the sudden beggary of its rich oppressors.[7] Later, the famished poor, driven desperate by the high costs of food, looted a warehouse stored with flour.[8]

Now, when the people learned that the bankers, as a retort to President Van Buren, had decided to suspend specie payments, all the passions of the common

[6] *New York Commercial Advertiser*, May 10, 1837.
[7] *Diary of Philip Hone.*
[8] *New York Commercial Advertiser*, Feb. 14, 1837.

folk raged to the surface. They feared starvation. They accused the aristocrats of robbing them of their small stores of money. On the morning of May 10, when the action of the bankers was known, the terror and rage of the people were indescribable. All that day, Wall Street was filled with distressed and angry workmen, artisans and small shopkeepers. They gathered before City Hall. Riots were feared. Troops were called out. The mayor of the city assembled a supply of ball cartridges in his office, in readiness for the soldiers assembled on duty in the Park.

Wall Street reeled under a wave of uncontrollable dismay. Bankers were torn by mutual hatreds. The people were fired with anger against them. The mob was a helpless victim of a cyclical catastrophe— the lowering cloud of an ended cycle!

THE PERFECT CYCLE

ALL things come to an end—even panics, after they have taken their toll from the gamblers and adventurers who produced them.

The men of the thirties paid their score.

Nicholas Biddle, the banking genius, whose vivid mind had engineered the wild movement, headed the list of losers.

Michigan, Lousiana, Mississippi and other States had created stocks to buoy up the paper notes of their local banks—paper floated upon paper. Biddle, who had attempted to corner cotton, confidently went to the rescue of the Southern States and banks. He took their securities, and operating through N. M. Rothschild & Sons of London, and Rothschild Frères of Paris, landed immense quantities on investors in England and on the European continent. This paper was snatched up at par by persons who had not yet discovered the tottering condition of American finance. Our country's financial reputation received a serious blow. More than 150 millions of European capital

66

was engulfed by the eventual repudiation of these securities.[1]

In 1841 came an exposure of the terrible condition of the once powerful United States Bank. Out of supposed assets of seventy-four millions, it could exhibit only twelve millions of active capital. Being compelled to refuse payments on drafts from New York, it went under and ended its career.

The dazzling Biddle had resigned from the Bank in 1839. He was indicted during the liquidation, but the indictment was quashed. "The idol of women, the favorite of Europe, the ornament of society and wielder of great power," now earned the title of "financial Lucifer." Friends who had once fawned upon him, cut him on the street.[2] He died in '44, insolvent and broken-hearted, at Andalusia, his beautiful country-seat on the banks of the Delaware.

J. L. & S. Josephs, Wall Street's leaders in the movement, whose downfall had precipitated the panic, were definitely ruined. Their liabilities were five millions. Even their office furniture had to be sold at auction. Moses Henriques, who at one time had been worth a million dollars on the firm's books, saved only a couple of houses, which he had settled

[1] James K. Medbery: *Men and Mysteries of Wall Street*, Boston, 1870.

[2] Edmund Clarence Stedman: *The New York Stock Exchange*, N. Y., 1905.

on his children.[3] The United States Bank later fore-
closed a mortgage for half a million on their ambitious real estate improvement of New Brighton, at
Fresh Pond, Staten Island.

The agency for the Rothschilds was assumed the
same year by a young man they had sent out from
Germany. His foreign air, dress and accomplish-
ments, brought him into contact with the young bucks
of the day. He mixed with such gay young fellows
about town as the Heywards, the Cuttings, the Cos-
ters, the Laights and the Livingstons. He aspired to
social and political influence, and became Grand
Sachem of Tammany Hall. His name was August
Belmont. He represented a coming generation. It
was to be guided by more subtle ways and better
foresight than had been exhibited by the performers
in the panic of '37.

The examples of Biddle and the Josephs brothers
swallowed up an army of their followers. But in the
end, as always, the public paid. No one escaped the
penalties caused by the lack of ready money. The
so-called "Jackson money" brought confusion and
bitter complaints. Companies and individuals, restaurant owners, grocers, barbers, all went into the
banking business on their own account. They issued

[3] *Stocks and Stock-Jobbing in Wall-Street*, N. Y., 1848.

shin-plasters, being forced to this step by the necessity for making small change for their customers.[4]

The cycle whose dénouement struck Wall Street in '37, is a perfect example of those outbursts which periodically descend upon it with stunning force.

How similar to the cycle which culminated in 1929. One is struck by the resemblance. Speculations in wild lands, like those in Florida, a century after. Bankers loaning their funds with equal liberality. The same optimists, dazzled by a future of their own creating.

With the reaction came similar consternation. Frightened crowds. Mutual accusations. Even the fall of stocks in the stable near William Street, presented its humble analogy to the deflation on the Exchange in '29.

This world of one hundred years ago lived under the same illusions, heedless of warning signals, until the day of atonement came with its panic,—the visitation supposed by the Greeks to have been sent by Pan, the god of huntsmen and shepherds.

One looks rather in vain for some of those many theories of the political economists. For certainly the specie troubles, the bank runs, the flow of gold to Europe, were merely the results, not the causal effects

[4] *N. Y. Commercial Advertiser*, May 18, 1837.

of the unbalanced efforts of the opportunists of the time to control staples and develop land.

To all appearances, the panic of '37 was the result of men's ventures. The men of '37 were blind to its approach. But the men of '29 were fully as blind, and a century of experience lay behind them.

Still, one can afford to withhold judgment. There is no need of being hasty in formulating an opinion. This was Wall Street's first panic. Others are to follow. It is only by comparing them that one may possibly discover that characteristic that all must possess in common.

III

THE GOLD STIMULANT

VII

THE cycle swinging in a fresh orbit, bringing revolutionary changes.

A multitude of new strategists, contrivers, adventurers, in full cry after ardent aspirations.

Wall Street in the fifties showed men strolling about, murmuring in suppressed excitement. They sported peculiar costumes, broad, reddish-brown felt hats, high boots, loose rough coats reaching to their knees. And while they strolled and murmured, they stared in shop windows at exhibits of knapsacks, gun slings, rubber suits, picks and gold sifters.[1]

In those years, steamers left their moorings daily for Chagres or San Francisco, while spectators on the crowded piers cheered them on. Obscure men, the future bonanza kings, were boarding the sailing ships: Mackay, the coming millionaire; those reckless but lucky boys, Flood and O'Brien; the merchant adventurers, Collis P. Huntington and Darius O. Mills.

Then the first ships came back with cargoes of gold dust and nuggets, bearing groups of rich and ragged

[1] *N. Y. Tribune*, January 30, 1849.

Californians, with stories of hardships, disasters, murders and deaths from cholera. The golden flood streamed in, pouring into the Port of New York at a rate of more than four millions a month, more than fifty millions a year.

Day after day these scenes were repeated as vessels came up from the Isthmus: the *Cherokee,* from Chagres, with a cargo worth more than two million dollars; the *Prometheus,* from Nicaragua, with a gold burden of nearly three millions; the *George Law,* from Panama, with one worth fourteen hundred thousand; the United States Steamship *Illinois,* with $1,700,000; the *Northern Light* from Aspinwall, with $1,688,000.

James Gordon Bennett rejoiced that the El Dorado of the old Spaniards was discovered at last; [2] but in the minds of others, this unexampled good fortune, which seemingly was to last forever, stirred feelings of uneasiness, if not alarm. "The gold of California," said Horace Greeley, "may strengthen and benefit us, or it may deprave and destroy us!" [3]

This new generation visioned the first great railroad promotions. One hundred thousand men, in New York City alone, were preparing to take up their line of march across the prairies and mountains

[2] *N. Y. Herald,* Dec. 9, 1848.
[3] *N. Y. Tribune,* Dec. 6, 1848.

74

to the alluring placers of California. Soon long emigrant trains were to cross the Western plains. Railroad construction was pushed forward with feverish activity.

Wall Street busily manufactured securities in these coming roads. They were sold at heavy discounts, and the entire country came forward as buyers. From the time of the gold discoveries, $700,000,000 was invested in railroad paper, but this sum largely represented foreign capital. Agents of Wall street financiers invaded European capitals, loaded down with railroad scrip. In London, Paris, Vienna, Berlin,—the chief centers of their operations, they lived in a style equal to that of the wealthiest nobles, scattering money with prodigal hands. Their dinners at Mivart's and the Clarendon, their Epicurean banquets at Tortoni's and the Maison Dorée, their splendid equipages and reckless extravagance combined to gild the bait which attracted many dupes.[4] For the railways thus exploited by these early super-salesmen, were being built into a distant Western wilderness, as though their mere appearance there would cause cities to spring to life and create traffic where none existed.

In these years of the early fifties, the New Haven and the Harlem railways jointly occupied a building

[4] *Herald*, Oct. 19, 1857.

in Hanover Street. From its doors one could see messengers emerging with armfuls of stock certificates, on the run to the Brokers' Board, to facilitate the keen speculation in the rails.

The president of these roads was a member of one of the proudest families in New York,—Robert Schuyler, grandson of Major-General Philip Schuyler, distinguished in the Revolution. He was the personal friend and financial representative of Commodore Vanderbilt, who was then organizing the Nicaragua Transit Company to compete with the Pacific Mail. Vanderbilt often observed that, in view of the manner of business conduct, he had more confidence in Robert Schuyler than in any other man.

Work continued late in the Hanover Street offices. Quite often there were conferences between Mr. Schuyler and Alexander Kyle, Jr., secretary of the Harlem road. When evening came, the social aristocrat, Schuyler, left, sometimes on foot, at others in his carriage, but always unaccompanied. He was a man close, contained and proud. His journey was not in the direction of his pretentious bachelor quarters uptown. His destination was to a world unknown to his fellow directors, Jonathan Sturges, William E. Worthen, Wyllis Blackstone or Vanderbilt and his other fashionable friends.

76

Wall Street had never seen such prosperous days. Registered sales at the Brokers' Board averaged more than 40,000 shares a session. Bankers generously forwarded speculation with free hands. They were ready to loan on almost any description of paper.[5] It is said of these marvelous times that brokers, with only $1,500 on deposit, drew checks for $100,000 and even $300,000, which were promptly certified by paying tellers. Financiers succumbed to the strain. Mining schemes, railway enterprises, guano speculations, sugar, cotton, lead operations sent men into insane asylums or brought life to a full stop.[6]

Amazing revelations now occurred. Officers of stock companies were exposed in issuing spurious shares. Managers of the Vermont Central Railway were driven to this extremity in order to supply the needs of their road. Officials of the Parker Vein Coal Company flooded the market with a fraudulent share issue of nearly five times the authorized capital. The checks of Simeon Draper, Jr., a prominent railroad banker, were dishonored; the Broadway Bank called his loans, and in his downfall he carried his brokers with him. Affairs of the Chicago & Mississippi Railroad next ruined Henry Dwight, Jr., another banker.

[5] *New York Day-Book*, D. Francis Bacon, Dec. 8-18, 1848.
[6] Medbery: *Men and Mysteries.*

77

Then came still more astonishing rumors to the Street. The New Haven directors were making mysterious investigations in the railroad offices in Hanover Street. An announcement was made of the failure of Schuyler & Company, the head of which was the distinguished financier, Robert Schuyler. At once Vanderbilt hastened to his friend's office. He handed him a check for $150,000, to help him out of his embarrassment. He offered him assistance to the extent of three millions. Schuyler had only to assure him that "all was right." But Schuyler turned aside and refused to speak.

A thunderbolt hit Wall Street next morning. A stock fraud was disclosed in New Haven that exceeded, in its enormity, all the previous railroad scandals. President Schuyler had fled to Canada, an absconder. He had actually forged stock in his own road to the tune of two millions. His mysterious absences from his bachelor quarters were explained. He had been living a double life for years. In another home he had a family under the assumed name of Spicer.[7]

The legal capital of the New Haven was three millions, but now, in the market, there was outstanding stock with a par value of five millions. On the Exchange, the road's shares dropped 23 points.

[7] *N. Y. Evening Post,* July 6, 1854.

Besides being the road's president, Schuyler had also been its transfer agent. Thus he had been able to conceal his emissions of fraudulent stock. He had swindled his close friend, Vanderbilt. He had obtained a loan from him of nearly $600,000, by pledging spurious shares.

Next day brought a discovery that more than five thousand shares of the Harlem road also had been fraudulently overissued. Alexander Kyle, Jr., confessed the responsibility. In the joint offices of the two roads in Hanover Street, the president of one road and the secretary of the other had been secretly swapping shares of their respective companies. They had gambled on the Exchange for a rise, but their stocks had dropped, because, with singular perversity, they had constantly supplied the market with larger and larger quantities of their forged shares.

Schuyler had also misappropriated $200,000 in Harlem railroad bonds. As Vanderbilt's agent, he had retained the money for himself. All these plundered sums had now been engulfed in the stock market.

A grave check came to credit and confidence. New Haven stockholders anxiously waited to learn whether their road was still solvent. Gouverneur Morris failed. He had endorsed Schuyler's notes, which he was unable to take up. Stock operators who had made loans on the road's securities became embarrassed. Many brokers suspended.

There was a robbery of $14,000 from the banking house of August Belmont, then minister to The Hague. William Paul, Belmont's cashier, advertised a reward for the capture of the thief. Later, Paul confessed to have stolen the money himself.[8] Henry Sheldon and three other directors of the Erie announced their suspensions. A run came to the Empire City Bank. In the Ocean Bank, McGuigan, a teller, stole $50,000.

In a bar-room, Thomas Howland, paying teller of the National Bank, was drinking deeply. In a drunken confidence, he divulged to the bank's porter that he was a defaulter for $70,000. The porter ran to tell the bank's president, James Gallatin. Howland was arrested. His pockets were stuffed with bills of exchange. He had been about to flee to Europe. A receiving teller looted the Market Bank of $25,000 and squandered it in the stock market. A detective lurked in a gambling saloon in Ann Street, watching the first bookkeeper of the Union Bank, Benjamin K. Brotherson. He notified the bank's officers that their employee was losing large sums at

[8] *N. Y. Evening Post*, July 13, 1854.

faro. Brotherson escaped, leaving forged balances to the size of $200,000.[9]

Gloom overhung Wall Street. The stock market was smashed. Banks called their loans right and left. Never had it seemed more difficult to obtain money. There were panics in Cincinnati and other cities, and word came from Indianapolis that there was scarcely a dollar in the State of Indiana save free bank paper.

California, within ten years, had produced gold dust and nuggets to the enormous value of 555 millions. Steamers were still arriving with their precious cargoes. But all this wealth—this gold—had become merely a commodity for export. On the discovery of the goldfields, Greeley had predicted that the treasure from California might prove a blessing or a source of depravity.

Wall Street had seen the names of great families dragged through the mud. Trusted heads of corporations had swindled investors in their own securities. This infatuation had spread like a malignant disease. It had inoculated minor officials and ruined them in speculations. A desire had been communicated in common to get rich swiftly. All strata of the community had been affected. Men differed only in their methods. Clerks had stolen huge sums

[9] *Ibid.*, Nov. 28, 1854.

from banks that employed them. They had flung everything away in mining offices and gambling hells. Credit was gone, confidence lost, and the country denuded of money.

Still the stately fleets steamed up from Aspinwall, freighted with their mocking millions.

Yet, until recently, the Street had been swooning in an ocean of wealth. Does prosperity breed panics, or do hard times produce them? The zenith came to Wall Street's riches in the years approaching 1929, but one saw trust companies plundered, public officials defaulting, bankers involved, judges disgraced. The downfall of moral sense was displayed in the exhibition of ambitious greed. Why question the economists? Let us proceed and judge for ourselves.

VIII

THE CATACLYSM OF '57

ALL this had brought on the panic.

Slowly gathering, the cycle reached its focal point and struck Wall Street on a morning in August, 1857.

Men, on passing an old monetary office, long familiar to the Street, were startled on seeing its doors shut. A curious crowd gathered. A card, pinned upon the doors, announced, in red ink, a death warrant for many brilliant hopes:

> TRANSFER BOOKS OF THE
> OHIO LIFE INSURANCE & TRUST COMPANY
> ARE CLOSED

Here, in the middle of the nineteenth century, the shares of a company had been manipulated to the highest pitch. "Their advance represented a discounted value of future dividends and earnings," to employ a sentence coined by our recent financial philosophers. These shares had won the confidence of investors, but the public had been hoaxed. The stock had been sold on false pretenses. The true condition of the company had been concealed.

We saw the same practice pursued in the late twenties of the twentieth century. In Wall Street, the years have brought no changes to this custom, but *it makes the market*.

Only a few days before the panic, Ohio Life & Trust shares had been selling at $102, and paying ten per cent. The sellers knew, though the buyers didn't, that the company had made imprudent advances to Western railroads. Now it was stranded on the rock of failure. Its liabilities were five million dollars. All the money was now gone. Nothing was left to depositors and stockholders but to bite their finger nails.[1]

The downfall of this company let loose upon the country unimaginable disaster. It heralded the cataclysm.

At first there was no outward indication of a crisis. Small groups of men, with thoughtful faces, talked in undertones, as they lingered about Lord's Court, where the Stock Board had established itself the year before.

The sheriff had taken possession of the books and papers of the Ohio Life & Trust. Its doors had now

---

[1] *Herald*, August 25, 1857.

been opened. Inquisitive persons peeped in at the deputy-sheriffs in charge. Some hours passed. The market broke heavily in the Lord's Court Exchange. Then the Street was stunned by news of a flood of failures.

Shocks and alarms continued. Newsboys ran through the financial district with wailing voices, hawking handbills containing public warnings against certain city banks. Stocks came out of every hole and corner. Brokers toppled down like so many loose bricks,—Clark, Dodge & Company, one of the strongest houses in the Street, and Beebe & Company, an old firm of bullion dealers, entangled in the affairs of the Ohio Life & Trust.

There were runs on the Metropolitan Bank and the Bank of Commerce. The Mechanics' Banking Association failed just as one of its clerks was caught red-handed in the act of embezzling $70,000.

Then came a lull. The Street had a breathing spell. But as merchants gathered at discount day, banks pushed their paper back upon them with scarcely an explanation. Mills closed. There was no money to pay their help. The commercial world seemed sweeping into illimitable ruin.

The paper inflation of the country was estimated at two thousand millions,—a much larger sum than all the gold currency derived from Australia and California combined.

On October 1, there was an abrupt and frightful stampede among the brokers in Lord's Court. Dozens broke as the market seemed to have no bottom. In despair, they turned on one another. Bull and bear came into close personal conflict. Fierce blows mingled with the ceaseless rapping of the president's hammer and the slaughter of every description of security.

A strange spectacle was witnessed on the morning of October 13. It resembled an occult vassalage of the people to some mysterious discipline. News spread like wildfire through New York City that five or six banks had closed their doors in Greenwich Street. Shopkeepers, business men of all sorts, emptied tills, cash drawers and money boxes. They hustled downtown to demand specie for paper. Bank depositors followed. Broadway stages were filled to overflowing.[2]

They poured into Greenwich Street. The front steps of banks were packed with those who had preceded them. Porters and policemen were unable to make themselves heard above the racket, but they pointed to ominous signs already posted at the doors: "This bank has suspended!"

[2] *Herald*, Oct. 12, 1857.

The Ocean, North River, Grocers', Bowery and East River banks had broken. Hour after hour brought fresh multitudes, breathless and pale. Mobs ran from bank to bank, looking for those that were still solvent. Billholders were already besieging banks on the Bowery and in Chatham Street. Riotous confusion prevailed before the Butchers' & Drovers' Bank at Grand Street.

Wall Street was nearly impassable in a congestion of alarmists, thieves, idlers, the curious, the unemployed. As the Marine Bank at Water Street went, mobs became more desperate. Each moment was freighted with bad news. Few checks were paid in gold over the counters. Banks handed out bills of different city institutions. The recipients, hastily assorting these, made their ways as quickly as they could to the issuing banks, where they presented them, demanding specie.

In the hurly-burly were groups arguing, expressing unbelief. One man boasted of the strength and solvency of the Market Bank. His few thousands deposited there he considered as safe as if they were in the United States Mint. A friend rushed up to ejaculate: "Have you heard the news?" "What news?" "The Market Bank is gone." "The devil you say!" and the depositor, with tense face and anxious eye, set off to ascertain the unbelievable fact.

The broad steps of the Merchants' Exchange were black with people. They were watching the run on the American Exchange Bank across the way, watching old David Leavitt come out upon the stoop, his gray head bare, shouting that the bank would keep on paying specie, yes, paying out to its last dollar, or so long as it had a drop of life-blood left.

Word then came that the Bank of New York had succumbed. It was the oldest bank in the city—the strongest that had yet failed.

Alarm subsided into silent despondency. The extent of the monetary disaster was beginning to be realized.

At the close of banking hours, with one exception, all the old-line Wall Street depositories were still solvent. But eighteen banks were broken in the city on that fatal October 13.

The crisis ended at last, for the associated banks suspended cash payments. The city resigned itself to accept bank notes as a circulating medium. The Chemical Bank, alone, continued to pay out gold.[8]

[8] *Herald*, Oct. 15, 1857.

IX

IN our post-panic days, it was the mood of those whom the stock market had disappointed, to drop from penthouses and skyscraper windows; to seek consolation in motor crashes, or to take nose-dives in their airplanes by freezing the controls. In the middle nineteenth century, our countrymen showed more resisting power.

Yet a socially well-to-do class that the years of high prosperity had produced was nearly extinguished by the crisis of '57. Families in the world of fashion, whose society had been courted, sank to lowly conditions.

Up and down Broadway drove a carriage drawn by a magnificent pair of horses. It exhibited the placard: "For Sale." It had been the property of a great drygoods merchant. A poor man forty years before, he had built up a trade extending into nearly every State in the Union, supplied by the productions of his ninety mills. Now the millions that had flowed through his hands were gone. His fine residence was to let. He had removed with his family to a neat, two-story house in the Seventh Ward, where he intended to live until his debts were paid.

But the strangest reversal of fortune had overtaken the once prosperous John Thompson. He was a Wall Street banker whose affairs had reached a singular success. He was a specialist in the complicated paper currency of the time. "Wild-cat" money was widely circulated. Bankers, merchants and tradesmen were accustomed to rely on his famous *Bank Note Reporter*. It was the authority on values of current and uncurrent bills issued by all the banks in the country. Leading financial institutions intrusted him with consignments of paper money for his expert appraisal. Agents in every State kept him posted on the constantly fluctuating values of paper currency.

Thompson's wealth had been accumulated rapidly. He astonished his fellow bankers by bidding for the entire issue of the latest State Loan,—$1,500,000. He paid for these bonds with apparent ease. It was understood that he had taken on some gigantic railroad enterprises, but when the Ohio Life & Trust went down, he went with it. The Street heard then that the Metropolitan Bank had obtained a warrant for his arrest. The charge was fraud in withholding securities and bank notes intrusted to his firm. After this, Thompson vanished entirely from the financial picture.

Less than a week after the crisis, an out-of-town banker visited Wall Street. He was eager to consult the onetime celebrated authority on current and uncurrent bank notes. For a long time he could not locate him. Finally, one of the financier's former employees hinted that he might be found at an address in Greenwich Street. Thither the visitor wended his way. Making inquiries in a ramshackle and forbidding building, he was told that no banker occupied the place, but it seemed that a man named Thompson, who made candles, could be found upstairs. He ascended a dingy flight of stairs. There the out-of-town banker was amazed on beholding the former great financier, wearing an apron, superintending the manufacture of candles from Breckenridge coal oil, and apparently as happy and as much at home in his new surroundings, as he had been in his luxurious banking parlors.[1]

Such was the stamina, resiliency and courage of our countrymen in the days of '57, their adaptability to new conditions, and resignation in the face of loss.

The imaginations and the ambitions of this generation had been stimulated by the gold discoveries. Gold production of the world was swollen from a previous average of nine millions, to one of 133 millions a year. This apparent good fortune revolu-

[1] *Herald*, Oct. 18, 1857.

91

tionized the life of the planet. It caused an un-heard-of stimulation of enterprise.

The extension of railways was a natural conse-quence. Men were quick to grab their opportunities. Hundreds of thousands migrated across a continent alive with perils. While these moved forward, the promoters stayed behind, to gamble on the uncertain fortunes of their fellows. Wall Street seethed with unbridled schemes. Bankers bestowed their credits upon them. All this led to an increasing ratio of frauds, and a deep social corruption. Unusual pros-perity has a way of causing such reactions.

The people of '57 wore the likeness of those of three-quarters of a century later. They imagined that the superabundance of riches would last forever, that it justified hopes without end, happiness ever-lasting.

Yet by the first half of the nineteenth century, all this wealth that had been dug from the earth in the form of gold, suddenly vanished. Notwithstanding the production of nine years, it had totally disap-peared from circulation and even from the vaults of banks.[2]

Indeed, more borrowed money had been spent, than the value of the entire golden flood. The glori-

[2] Conant: *History of Modern Banks of Issue.*

92

ous prospect had lasted but for the brief period of the cycle's life.

It seems reasonable to assume that not economic causes, but the promotions of optimistic men, caused the panic of '57. The sudden disappearance of specie, the embarrassment of the banks, the outward flow of gold, were the consequences of this super-optimism.

It had led the managers of the Ohio Life & Trust to pay ten per cent dividends, while its assets had already been lost in bad loans. It led to the spurious share issues of the Vermont Central; of the Parker Vein Coal Company. It carried all away in common: Schuyler, forging the New Haven's stock; Kyle, that of the Harlem road; it ran the entire gamut of human society, from Paul, Belmont's cashier, down to Howland, the paying teller, Brotherson, the bank's bookkeeper,—all those scouts of lesser note, who became defaulters, thieves and gamblers. They had never before been marked with the sign of roguery. Ill-timed pawns. In the whirlwind they had maneuvered their own destruction.

Men, and they alone, seem to have been the consistent originators of this panic. As in '37, as in a century later, one seems to see the human element predominant in the cataclysm.

93

IV.

THE RAILROAD CONTRIVERS

X

ANOTHER great opportunist rose in the late
sixties and the early seventies. He was the
chief performer in their exploits and their unsettlements.

This was Jay Cooke, in his cape coat and flowing
beard, a theatrical but patriotic genius, the financier
of the Civil War in his banking house in Philadelphia, when Wall Street bankers failed the country.
His talents for publicity originated those methods of
marketing emergency government bonds [1] which were
later copied and elaborated in the days of the World
War.

Cooke was a great banker through stormy and
tempestuous years. He was the country's foremost
moneyed man after the close of the Civil War.

Settlers were pouring into the "New Northwest."
Roads leading to the Red River Valley were covered
with emigrant wagons. Caravans traveled to the
fertile regions of Northern Minnesota. Campfires

[1] Ellis Paxon Oberholtzer: *Jay Cooke, Financier of the Civil
War.* Phila., 1907, Vol. I, pp. 162, 165.

97

were seldom permitted to die out. Fresh trains of emigrants arrived almost as soon as their predecessors had resumed the march.[2]

A horde of organizers plunged into the adventure of building metal highways. Their promotions were stimulated by bond subsidies and huge land grants. Perils faced these undertakings. But they were built boldly and with a rapidity which demanded deep outlays of money. In fact, the absorption of capital in large enterprises during the ten years prior to '73 was as great as had been the waste in wars.[3] In the last five of those years, nearly 30,000 miles of road were built. Their cost was about one billion, four hundred millions.[4]

Jay Cooke was the undoubted leader in such undertakings. He was capable and confident, fortified with a great, hearty, open manner, and he seemed invincible. He was now engaged in the project which he believed would add to his fame,—the carrying through of the Northern Pacific Railroad, from Lake Superior to distant Puget Sound. He had picked up large amounts of stock in this bankrupt enterprise at from 12 to 15 cents on the dollar, before announcing his intentions. Now 455 miles of road were

[2] *Commercial and Financial Chronicle*, July 1, 1871.
[3] Conant: *Hist. Modern Banks of Issue*, p. 653.
[4] Henry V. Poor: *Manual of the Railroads of the U. S.*, 1874-75.

already in operation, but the whole vast enterprise was entirely dependent upon his individual efforts.

Among those venturesome contrivers who followed Cooke's example in the active upswing in railroad securities, were the promoters of the Union Pacific. Under the corporate title of the Crédit Mobilier, they began the construction of this road. Managers of a moneyed corporation in Pine Street, known as the New York Warehouse & Security Company, a strong institution, were tempted, by offers of heavy commissions, to finance the Missouri, Kansas & Texas road. The underwriting and flotation of securities of the Canada Southern road were undertaken by Kenyon, Cox & Company, with which Daniel Drew had once been identified.

But now the perils which faced the engineering work in building the metal highways were to be paralleled by their financing. In the years that had just passed, national resources had been emptied upon great conflicts like water. The Civil War had cost some six billions. The Franco-Prussian War nearly three billions.

Squalls were now threatening. Infatuated promotions had caused credit inflation. The amount of railroad paper afloat was rising to dangerous heights. Paper circulation had increased to $750,000,000. In '71, the Chicago fire destroyed values to the tune of

99

150 millions, and the Boston fire, the year following, increased the loss in real property.

Scandal overwhelmed the Crédit Mobilier. Oakes Ames, prominently identified with the concern, had distributed, as a member of Congress, large amounts of Union Pacific stock amongst his fellow members. This had been done for the purpose of obtaining favorable legislation for the road. It was disclosed that the directors had taken over from dummies, contracts for the construction of the railway line. The contracts were grossly extravagant, and the profits correspondingly high.

Ames was expelled from the House of Representatives. He had previously failed for nearly eight millions.

The Missouri, Kansas & Texas was unable to meet its loans. Thereupon the New York Warehouse & Security Company went under. One million and a quarter of its paper was afloat.

Kenyon, Cox & Company went bankrupt, involved in the affairs of the Canada Southern.

A series of failures, embezzlements and peculations came to light as a result of railroad hazards. Barton & Allen failed. They were respectively nephew and grandson of Commodore Vanderbilt. The Commodore refused to help them because he condemned speculation. The collapse of J. L.

Brownell was followed by that of Legrand Lockwood, an old house, established back in '42. Several savings banks were ruined.

The Bull's Head Bank closed, the Atlantic Bank succumbed, its cashier having embezzled its available assets of $400,000, and the Brooklyn Trust Company went into receivership, owing to a large overdraft of its president, Mills, who drowned himself off Coney Island.

Jay Cooke had been negotiating the sale of fifty millions of Northern Pacific bonds in Germany. His plans were frustrated by the Franco-Prussian War. He was compelled to place the bonds in this country. But the market was by this time overloaded.

A frightful depression ensued with an abruptness never before signalizing such an event.[5]

[5] Thomas P. Kane: *The Romance and Tragedy of Banking*, N. Y., 1923.

XI

MORNING of September 18, 1873.
In his fairy palace, "Ogontz," in the
Chelten Hills, eight miles from Philadelphia, Jay
Cooke was at breakfast with President Grant. Suddenly the private telegraph wire running to his secluded mansion brought him shocking intelligence.
His Wall Street house, burdened down with huge
collaterals that had become unmarketable, had announced its suspension in New York.[1]

Cooke stifled his agitation. He made excuses to
his distinguished guest. He ordered out his carriage,
and with gloom in his soul, he was driven to his
historic firm in Third Street, Philadelphia. Tears
came to the old man's eyes. He sorrowfully gave a
signal.[2]

The creaking doors of the dismal old institution,
through which had flowed the hundreds of millions
that had paid our soldiers in the Civil War, swung
shut.

The banker's Washington house, and the First

---

[1] Oberholtzer: *Jay Cooke.*   [2] *Ibid.*

National Bank, of that city, which he controlled, soon closed.

So incredible was Cooke's downfall to Philadelphia, that a policeman, hearing a newsboy shouting, "All about Jay Cooke's failure!" indignantly arrested the lad.[3]

When Cooke went down, he carried the financial world with him.

The dynamic visitation of the panic of '73 came to Wall Street that same day.

On the floor of the New York Stock Exchange, as its president announced the failure of Jay Cooke, his words were drowned in an uproar.

Had Cooke failed? Who, then, could be reckoned solvent?

It was an age of unrestrained emotions. Men gave full play to their feelings. Stocks tumbled, and Western Union lost ten points in as many minutes. It is authentically recorded that traders on the floor who saw themselves broken in an instant, tore their hair and ran about as if mad. They shrieked, and jostled others who had equally gone mad.[4]

Cooke's financial house stood at the corner of Nassau and Wall Streets. There, men were seen hustling anxiously up the steps to the banking floor. They bore small slips of paper in their hands. The

[3] *Ibid.*   [4] *Herald,* Sept, 19, 1873.

next moment they reappeared, downcast and crest-
fallen. Their non-success in cashing drafts was
only too plainly visible in their faces.

The desk of one of the bank's managers still exhibited an emblazoned sign:

```
A SURE AND SAFE INVESTMENT:
NORTHERN PACIFIC 7-30'S, AS GOOD AS
            GOVERNMENTS!
SECURED BY MORTGAGES AND LAND GRANTS
```

The crisis had transformed the brokers into mad-
men.

It churned up the wild and sullen resentment of
the mob.

On learning that Jay Cooke had been ruined by his
great promotion, a screaming, gesticulating crowd
gathered at the Nassau Street corner. Rough-looking
men peered through the windows, invaded the base-
ment, insultingly accosted the partners and clerks who
showed themselves.

Then a semi-circle of police was drawn about the
building.

In an avalanche, failures swept the Street. Rich-
ard Schell and Robinson & Suydam went under.
The New York & Oswego Midland Railroad de-

faulted on its bonds, and George Opdyke, its president, suspended.

All looked to Commodore Vanderbilt. They hoped he would appear as savior, as he had done on Black Friday, in Jay Gould's gold speculation of '69, when he saved the day in Centrals by throwing ten millions of money on the market.

But that evening in his home in Fourth Street, the Commodore shrugged his shoulders as he observed: "I am a friend of the iron road, but building railroads from nowhere to nowhere at public expense, is not a legitimate undertaking." [5]

The following day opened gloomy. The sky was dark with a pelting rain.

Wall Street, from Broadway to Hanover, was black with humans. Victims of an emotional cataclysm, they plodded through the mud to the environs of disaster.

Brokers, clerks and messengers flew on desperate errands. Men wore bewildered expressions, as though some mysterious portent were abroad, which they failed to understand.

High on the stone balustrades of the Sub-Treasury, spectators had balanced themselves. Under the shelter of umbrellas, they curiously contemplated this

[5] Stedman: *N. Y. Stock Exchange.*

scene,—an enigma to will and intellect, an incomprehensible destiny: the dark drama of '73.

On 'Change, a cluster of gas jets illumined the murky atmosphere. The board room of that time had a noble altitude. The great vaulted roof sprang gracefully to a focal point in the ceiling, whose surface was covered with a brilliant flourish of colors.

Behind the railed desk stood the board's president. To right and left of him, large blackboards displayed in chalk marks the swiftly changing quotations. In the center of the wide floor stood a small table bearing a basket of flowers. About this raged mad confusion. Rock Island was breaking in terrific fashion. Pacific Mail tumbled, and Central and Wabash were being tossed from hand to hand. In the gallery, spectators watched aghast. Through open windows, the chorus of voices swept into the wet and crowded street.

When Saturday came, no sooner were the doors of the Exchange thrown open, than pale-faced brokers, impotent slaves to the dominant catastrophe, rushed out upon the floor. Few of them had had a night of rest. They resembled a mob of dissipated revelers, desperately under the weather. Two failures were made known in swift succession. Then the president announced that the Exchange was closed. A shout echoed from the roof. A wild rush followed to the doors.

But there was no check to the fast-recurring announcements of suspensions. The days seemed subject to the decisions of a pitiless will.

The secretary of the Union Trust defaulted for $400,000, and the institution closed. After sustaining a run, the National Trust in Broadway did likewise, and was imitated by the Bank of the Commonwealth, on whom Haight & Company had overdrawn their account by $225,000.

Firms which had resisted the worst of former crises were being submerged. The choicest securities had depreciated 20 to 30 per cent. Bankers in the Clearing House, then situated over the Bank of New York, decided to issue $10,000,000 in certificates, to be used instead of legal tenders.

On Monday, Henry Clews suspended, having overdrawn his account by $165,000. As the firm demanded an additional $135,000, the Fourth National Bank refused to clear for it and threw out its checks. There were runs upon the savings banks. Thirty-six firms had suspended or failed within the few days of the panic.

The Exchange was closed for more than a week. While its members were forbidden to trade, the curb brokers, whose vantage ground was the street, with the azure dome of heaven for a roof, monopolized the breadth of Broad Street. Sly members of the Stock Board, with the penalty of expulsion hanging over them, slipped in and out, occasionally decoying speculators to their offices, or flinging stock offerings over the heads of the crowd.

Six weeks of disorganization and downfall culminated with the failure of the great Sprague enterprises. Their paper went to protest. They had employed 10,000 hands in mills and print works and mowing machine companies.

A million wheels were checked throughout the country. In New York, the unemployed numbered 40,000. Rents fell 30 per cent.

The Northern Pacific went bankrupt. Jay Cooke vanished from existence as a firm. Seventy-two railway corporations were in default. Overdue interest on their bonds amounted to $218,000,000, or 13 per cent of the funded debt of the metal highways.

XII

THE HORN SILVER MINE

ALL the ponderous volumes evolved by astute professors, all the profound theories of banking experts to the contrary, the events of '73 once more seem to teach the lesson that the origin of panics is to be found not in economic laws, but in human action.

The men of the seventies were spurred on by the potentialities of railroad promotion. Their eyes were set only upon this goal. They pushed forward without a let-up. They ignored imposing obstacles, destructive wars that cost billions, prodigious fires in great cities.

Swayed by the lures of fame, greed, loot, by the allied motives of acquisition, blind to consequences in the face of calamities, they battled through the wrecks of the crumbling era.

One saw Jay Cooke chasing the *ignis fatuus* of the Northern Pacific promotion, that was to wreck the big Villard pool of a later generation. Oakes Ames and his confederates involved themselves in the rogueries of the Crédit Mobilier. Bankers were sunk in their underwritings of the Katy and the Canada Southern. Barton, Allen, Brownell, Legrand Lockwood, were entangled in railway share speculations, while the bank president plunged to his death in Coney Island's surf, and the cashier embezzled the assets of the Atlantic Bank.

Honest but misdirected efforts, plain swindles, blind gambles, bald thefts, all lead to the same conclusions. Scenes ensued with which one is growing familiar: stocks falling on the exchanges, uproar and consternation, the Pan-complex of crowds paralyzed by the dismaying riddle.

The panic of '37 had resulted from the confident hopes of men who backed land and cotton ventures; that of '57 was due to men who were overwhelmed in the unsettlements caused by an unheard-of influx of gold metal; that of '73 resulted from the schemes of men who succumbed to the hypnosis of railway projection.

Yet, out of the ruin and wreckage of each cataclysm, there remained something accomplished. The land speculators of '37 left behind them foundations, even in the phantom towns of the wilderness. The argonauts of '57 left trails behind their visionary projects. The promoters of '73 inaugurated a country's development before failure overtook them.

After the downfall,—recovery. There may be a

constructive secret behind the shadow of great panics. All may not be calamity. It may yet be proved that "the riches of nations can be measured by the violence of the crises they endure." [1]

This country had accumulated, in '73, some forty millions of inhabitants, which was more than three times the number existing in the days of '37. From now on, as populations grow, one shall see our panics expand in force and volume.

Years after the derangements of '73 had spent themselves, an old man, whose long hair, side-whiskers and beard flowed silvery-white to the collar of his old-fashioned cape coat, was to be seen wandering through Wall Street. He seemed be-wildered. He was looking up some half-remembered trail.

Finally the old man dropped into the offices of the Union Pacific Railroad. There he presented his name. He was at once admitted to the private office of Sidney Dillon, the president. Beside the latter sat a small man, with coal black beard and eyes.

In his biography of Jay Cooke, Ellis Paxon Ober-holtzer recalls the episode.

"How are you, Mr. Cooke," exclaimed Dillon, with a smile.

[1] Clément Juglar: *Des Crises Commerciales et De Leur Retour Périodique*, Paris, 1889.

III

The aged financier scrutinized the speaker, but he could not remember that they had ever met before.

But the railway chief reminded him of a long-forgotten incident. It related to the distant past, when Dillon was embarrassed, and Cooke had advanced him $20,000. "I was in trouble then, and you staked me," said the head of the Union Pacific. "I shall always remember that, Mr. Cooke. What can I do for you? Whatever you say shall be done," and he introduced his companion, an influential director in the railroad company,—Jay Gould.

Cooke promptly unrolled his maps and presented his case with some of that power of fascination with which of old he had compelled men to believe in him in spite of themselves. He related how, since his failure, he had put $3,000 into the Bonanza or Horn Silver Mine, in Utah. He had just returned from a visit to the property. In order to develop it, it was necessary to construct 176 miles of railway.

To his joy, Gould and Dillon assented to his proposal.

"With us three men," observed Cooke, with beaming eyes, as he gathered up his documents, "is there the least occasion for a written agreement?"

"No," was Gould's abrupt response. "You can go right ahead with your plans. We will take the remaining half interest, and supply you with the money."

And the verbal contract was kept. The road was completed, and Cooke, so long as he lived, when others spoke ill of Gould, delighted in relating this friendly incident.

Cooke's silver mine proved of exceptional value. His income, from the share he held, aggregated $80,000 a year. He sold his interest later for nearly a million dollars. The sum enabled him to regain possession of his old home in the Chelten Hills,— "Ogontz"—from which his creditors had driven him. He lived there to the ripe age of 84.

V

THE GAMBLING BANKERS

XIII

MEN OF THE EIGHTIES

AN altered world, this Wall Street of the eighties. Gone was that fierce hatred between the common people and the aristrocratic Whigs of '37. Those two rabid classes had disappeared. They were scarcely a memory.

The unrestrained emotions of '73 had calmed and settled.

Sons of the gold adventurers of the early fifties were now numbered among Wall Street's commanders.

For the first time in sixteen years, gold shipments were returning to the United States. Huge American grain crops had brought prosperity. Financiers delightedly manufactured and set afloat new securities, whose values were advancing.

A fresh crop of promoters and contrivers responded to the call of unchained aspirations. They were the planners and strategists whose hazardous operations were to introduce the panic of '84.

First and foremost amongst them was a financial operator of superior ability,—George Ingraham

Seney. He fought toward his objectives without scruples. He devoted the surplus loot taken in battle to his art collections. He built the Brooklyn hospital which bears his name.

Seney contrived a great fortune by means of a conscienceless combination,—the Seney Syndicate. Its greatest venture had been the projection and building of the notorious "Nickel Plate." This had been a defiance to William H. Vanderbilt, then successor to the fortune of his noted father. Vanderbilt had to buy the Nickel Plate to protect his Lake Shore & Michigan Southern, which it paralleled and threatened to ruin.

This deal netted a personal profit of $1,500,000 to Seney.

Through his Syndicate, Seney got control of the Ohio Central, the East Tennessee, the Virginia & Georgia and the Rochester & Pittsburg railways. He had a juggler's talent. He organized and reorganized all these properties. He devised share issues, which he sold cheaply but widely, on high promises. In this he did not have the present-day advantages of the movietone or the microphone. But he utilized advertising, which was then becoming a science.

The powerful Metropolitan Bank, with fifteen millions in resources, of which he was the head, was the machine with which Seney set his schemes in motion. The Exchange house of Nelson Robinson & Company, managed by his two sons and his son-in-law, and in which he was a special partner, financed the railways of the Syndicate.[1]

Seney, launching out furiously into the unknown, was a plaything of that destiny which is not so blind and inevitable as one imagines.

Another banker, all-unsuspected, was to be a performer in the coming stageplay. James D. Fish was a sporting financier. He had a ruddy, jovial face and fine bright eyes. Although in the middle sixties, he was lively in his habits. He was a club-frequenter, an after-dinner toastmaster. He was popular among shipping and commercial men, who owned stock in the Marine National Bank, with its five millions in resources, over which he had presided for twenty-six years.

Old Fish, with his solid reputation and his personal fortune of two millions, was to become mere fishing bait for a slim young fellow, with a pale and meager face, who was cursed with certain mysterious gifts with which so many an audacious newcomer contrives to plague the Street. This chap had floated down to Wall Street in '78. He applied for a job to the Produce Exchange. One of its officers had been a friend of his father, a Baptist minister up in Geneseo.

[1] Stedman: *N. Y. Stock Exchange.*

He got the job, but he secretly despised it. He immediately quadrupled his salary by gambling in memberships of the Exchange.

Now Ward, this youth of 27, had a deceitfully unassuming manner and extraordinary persuasive powers. Old, astute financiers, expert in arts of sharp-bargaining, fell helpless in his presence.[2]

Ward craved the possession of capital in a world where it was the sole means of getting ahead, and he scouted around for a moneyed backer. He found him in the person of old banker Fish, who was more than twice his age. The young phenomenon soon inveigled the head of the Marine National in a web of stock and real estate speculations.[3]

Ward had resigned from the Produce Exchange to take a desk in a broker's office. Now his neurotic mind led him to plan the execution of a much greater objective. In the end, this was to bring Wall Street in ruins about his ears.

It was a generation of youthful strategists. Another banker played his part in producing the panic of '84. He rose to prominence not by his own efforts, but through parental pride and indulgence. This was John C. Eno. He was blessed, or rather cursed, with an attractive but ardent temperament. At the untried age of 26, he was made president of the

[2] Stedman: *N. Y. Stock Exchange.* [3] *Ibid.*

Second National Bank. This was put over through the influence of his opulent father, Amos F. Eno. The latter owned the Fifth Avenue Hotel. The bank was situated in this building. Its depositors constituted the wealthiest families in the city.

Through a maneuver of the youthful president, the bank's collaterals were deposited in a Wall Street safety vault, because its lodgments were loaned out chiefly to brokers, and so, in order to accommodate borrowers, it was imperative for the susceptible youth to frequent the financial district daily. Here, through contacts with the big schemers and operators of the Street, he was initiated into the science of speculation. With great funds at his command, Eno's vivid imagination, stimulated by whisperings of his gambling friends, unfolded vistas of immense moneyed conquests, which would make him the leading financial figure of his day.

It was distinctive of these years that even the most conservative financiers were drawn into their complex. In William Street was an old-fashioned counting-room,—that of Matthew Morgan's Sons. It was one of the oldest banking houses in the city. The managing member, Henry Morgan, was conspicuous in the financial district for his gruff manners, his good nature and his congenital horror of anything that resembled stock gambling.

121

Led on by a supposed knowledge of the property, whose potentialities fascinated him, Henry Morgan had interested himself in Denver & Rio Grande. He had bought the shares at a very low figure. Then began Jay Gould's bull campaign of '81. The cautious old banker was swept off his feet by the spectacle of the price of $112 to which this road's stock was advanced. Convinced that his attitude was justified, he backed his good judgment by entering the foremost ranks of the plungers.

The insidious influence of the cycle was emphasized furthermore, in the fact that old Russell Sage, the craftiest man in Wall Street, with the reputation of being the most far-sighted of its financiers, was carried along in the belief that the market's advance would continue with unabated force. He backed this conviction as heavily as the horde of his illustrious successors did in 1929. The renowned dealer in "privileges" had been selling "puts" through every brokerage concern in the Street. Sage's "puts" were now in every hand. Not only in the financial district of New York, but also in moneyed circles of Boston, Philadelphia and other Eastern cities. He still sold them freely, by millions and yet more millions. He was operating on the strength of past experiences. He was confident that his keen judgment was correct.

XIV

DURING these auspicious times, at ten o'clock every business morning, Wall Street had grown accustomed to seeing a carriage driven up to the main entrance of the nine-storied United Bank Building, at the corner of Wall Street and Broadway. A man would then emerge, short and thick in body, with a close-clipped, grayish beard and a sphinx-like countenance. He wore a bow tie, high collar and a tall silk hat. He was known to all the country,—in fact, to all the world.

The man would stop on the sidewalk to light the historic cigar, black, rank and poisonous; for he was the most appalling smoker of his time.

As this man would take the preliminary puffs at his weed, he presented a picture of one contented with himself and all creation. After a career spent on battlefields, that led to the White House, he at last was happy. Honors had come, and glory. But money had always had its singular fascination. He had long coveted a fortune that would place his family beyond the chance of future poverty.

And now illusion had arrived. He had shown the world that he could be more than a mere soldier. He and his boys already possessed millions of undivided profits in the house of Grant & Ward.

In his momentary pause, the man's thoughts lingered on this miracle.

It may be of interest to recapitulate, in the General's mind, the singular circumstances by which all this had come to pass. His son, "Buck" Grant, had had the good fortune to meet and become associated with one whom he considered among the most brilliant financiers of the Street. This was Ferdinand Ward, whose successes had already insured him the title of "Young Napoleon."

The father thought it a lucky omen that the two youths were of nearly the same age, and that similar inclinations had drawn them together. Ulysses S. Grant, Jr., had married the only daughter of Senator Chaffee, Colorado mine owner. The Senator had presented the bride with a wedding gift of $400,000. With this capital, Buck had been enabled to join Ward in organizing the firm of Grant & Ward. The popular banker, James D. Fish, had become their silent partner.[1]

In General Grant's opinion, the firm possessed a sound financial foundation. He, himself, had suc-

[1] Stedman: *N. Y. Stock Exchange.*

cumbed to the strange personal magnetism which Ward seemed to exercise at will. The General and his other son, Jesse, each put $50,000 into the house. A third son, Frederick, joined the combination.[2]

Under the hypnosis of the Young Napoleon, the entire Grant family had embarked to follow in the wake of his rising star.[3]

Ferdinand Ward created in men's minds the fiction that he was a genius. "He overflowed all bounds by the force of a magnificent self-delusion; he was a juggler, who threw mists before your eyes—you had no time to detect his fallacies."

Ward had been quick to recognize the financial value of a distinguished name when fate led Buck into his toils. And Ward, the beguiler, actually rose as a luminary in the Street. He speculated with the firm's capital in the stock market that was rising in those cheerful, prosperous days. Luck stood with him in the first few years of the firm's existence. Through his audacities, the house appeared to flourish. In two years he had supposedly made potential profits of $2,500,000. His partners credited him with infallible judgment. They left the entire management in his hands. So marched the sequence of fatalities. So this macabre figure developed his futile operations.

[2] *Ibid.*   [3] *Ibid.*

Once General Grant had placed his trust in a man, that confidence could be shaken by nothing short of an earthquake. Totally inexperienced in business, he implicitly trusted his son, Ulysses. The latter, quite ignorant of the ways of Wall Street, relied entirely upon Ward. The mystery remains how poor old Fish, with his unblemished past, continued blind to danger.

Ward had really no speculative capacity. His abilities were of a mediocre order. His sole gift lay in his singular power to deceive. With the money of others at his command, he was swept ahead under the happy market auspices, to which the prevailing good times had given birth.

But the secret weakness of the house soon was known to the underworld of the Street. Its prestidigitators, thimbleriggers, beach combers, got Ward under their thumbs. They jockeyed and bamboozled him. His dealings always turned against him now. He plunged in mining shares, but they added to his losses. He was buying at top prices as a bear movement set in. He failed in ingenuity to meet the changed conditions. Then he covered his losses by turning rogue.

When luck turned against Ward, he invented a scheme which involved the use of General Grant's name as a decoy in a vast swindle. He induced men of means to deposit money with the firm. He represented that big profits were coming from Government contracts privately obtained through the General's influence. Of course, all this was to be kept a profound secret.

Ward gave receipts for such loans, and due bills for prospective profits, of which the following is a specimen:

Feb. 1, 1884.

This is to certify that we have this day received from Captain E. Spicer, Jr., $50,000; which we are to invest for him, and we agree to return him said $50,000 May 15, 1884, together with $5,000 profit.

Grant & Ward.

Ward was psychologist enough to know that so fast as he handed over the supposed dividends, his customers would hurry to re-invest in his "contracts." The latter were merely fictions of his neurotic mind. He was playing for time, for the market to turn in his favor.

But the sums Ward raised at such ruinous rates, simply plunged him into further difficulties. Then he began to discount the firm's notes. He paid as high as thirty per cent to "persons whom Grant & Ward desired to favor!" Of the money so obtained,

127

as he afterward admitted, he paid back to the lenders in short periods, not less than one-fifth in "discounts and profits." This insane system he kept up for nearly two years. He constructed a pyramid of liabilities that he could never hope to liquidate.

But the young contriver still kept up the fiction that the house was in possession of surplus millions. Having exhausted all shifts and ruses for providing fresh money, he actually fell back upon his deluded partners. Without weakening their confidence in his operations, he induced them to raise additional amounts of capital.

"Buck" Grant borrowed $500,000 from his indulgent father-in-law, Senator Chaffee, to pour into the limitless coffers of the house. General Grant, persuaded that a temporary emergency had arisen, was induced to appeal to William H. Vanderbilt for a loan of $150,000. The General took this step with natural reluctance. Vanderbilt consented to advance him the money as a personal loan. But the great financier took occasion to observe that he had small faith in Grant's young partner, Ferdinand Ward.[4]

Meanwhile, from his Marine Bank, credulous old Fish had been cozened into handing over to the Young Napoleon the stupendous sum of $4,144,000, mostly on the firm's unprotected notes.

[4] Stedman: *N. Y. Stock Exchange.*

Such was the status of affairs when morning opened on May 6, 1884.

The carriage, as usual, arrived before the United Bank Building.

This time, General Grant was seen emerging on crutches. He was still disabled from a fall sustained some months before.[5]

Grant was titular president of a Mexican railway company on the seventh floor. But before going up in the elevator, it was an invariable custom of his to stop and chat with his partners on the ground floor. So he hobbled slowly and unsuspectingly into the offices of Grant & Ward.

On the General's entrance, Spencer, the firm's cashier, looked up from the news ticker with a startled face.[6]

The cashier had long had fears that the house was in an irregular way. As market prices continued to fall, persons who had made loans were demanding return of their funds. Such payments were being delayed.

The cashier's suspicions were now confirmed. He was reading an alarming message, which, at that moment, was being ground out on the news ticker:

[5] Ulysses S. Grant: *Personal Memoirs.*
[6] Hamlin Garland: *Ulysses S. Grant, His Life and Character.*

129

*The big iron doors of the Marine National
Bank had just been closed. Policemen, stationed before them, were keeping back the
crowd. At the Clearing House, the bank had
been unable to make good a difference of $550,-
000! Old Mr. Fish, its president, had shut
himself up in a private room in the Clearing
House. He was besieged there by the bank's
directors. They were his friends, the shipping
men, who owned its stock. Fish refused to
meet them!*

Spencer felt himself incapable of announcing the
disaster. At that moment, Ulysses S. Grant, Jr.,
rushed into the room. "Well, Buck, how goes it?"
cheerily asked the General. The son, white-faced,
distracted, his head still ringing with the tidings of
the blow that had fallen upon the house, exclaimed
abruptly, without a softening word: "Father, the
Marine Bank has failed. Everything is gone. We'll
never get a cent back from Grant & Ward!"

For a few moments the old man faced the others.
His eyes penetrated to the bottom of his fear-stricken
son's despair. Then he hunched his crutches about,
slowly, uttering not a single word. He left the
quarters of Grant & Ward, to be seen there no more.

The suspension of Grant & Ward was formally

announced. Young Napoleon had fled. Schedules showed liabilities of nearly $17,000,000. Assets were represented by a bare $67,000. The firm's accounts were confused. No cash book or journal had ever been kept.

XV

THE CONJUNCTURE OF 1884

THE panic of '84 occurred in a transition period of history.

It struck with unexpected suddenness and left its victims stunned and dazed.

There had been few symptoms of forewarning. Bankers, usually the first to sense a coming storm, were caught as unawares as they were in the collapse of 1929.

Even old Russell Sage had misjudged his market in "puts and calls." For the first time in a long and cautious career, he found himself in serious predicaments.

The downfall of Grant & Ward came as a stroke of destiny. It uncovered a whole series of huge and sinister thefts and calamitous speculations. It destroyed the reputations of a score of men notable in the railway and banking worlds.

That day named in financial history as the "Grant & Ward panic," arrived on May 14. It was accompanied by the now familiar concomitants of the somber phenomenon.

THE CONJUNCTURE OF 1884

Gathering in upper Manhattan Island, streaming across Brooklyn Bridge, and arriving by the Jersey City ferryboats, morbid crowds, driven by despondent fears, sought distraction or amusement in the precincts of Wall Street.

On that day, a spectator, who viewed them from the steeple of Old Trinity, described them as massing in lines through Broadway and the length of Wall Street, like regiments of an army of beetles. Black hats shone and glistened in the sun. He could distinguish the newsboys rushing about. The traveling stages, which parted the throngs in waves. To the onlooker perched on high, the scene presented a surface black with humans. It was turbulent but soundless. Its noises failed to reach him.

Pushing his difficult passage through this jumbled mob of bank depositors, flash men, traders, mechanics, thieves and detectives, was George I. Seney. This notable financier had spent a sleepless night. With one of those abrupt changes, of which the stock market affords so many lurid instances, his forceful promotions had met with a sudden reversal. The Seney Syndicate found itself entangled in a bad plight. Its loans were being called. Its securities were unmarketable. Their values were falling to nothing.

The directors of the Metropolitan Bank had already become alarmed by the multitude of Seney's ventures. He had promised them that he would end all connection with his railroads. Before he could make good this assurance, he was called upon to fight a hostile market and respond to heavy money drains.

On this morning, red-eyed and haggard, Seney already knew in his heart that the disasters that had already occurred, were bringing his high banking and speculative structure toppling about his ears. He fought his way to the corner of Pine Street and Broadway. He slipped through a private entrance into the Metropolitan Bank. Here he hastily summoned a meeting of directors. By eleven o'clock, all were assembled behind the locked doors of the board room.

But already the intelligence was racing through Wall Street that Nelson Robinson & Company had suspended payments, owing nearly two millions. The close relations between this house and the Metropolitan Bank were only too well known. Seney, silent partner of the brokerage firm, owned three-fourths of the bank's stock.

A quarter of an hour later, the bank's cashier emerged from the secrecy of the board room and whispered to the paying teller. The latter at once brought down the slide of his wicket with a bang.

Through the wire screen, the assembled customers were informed that the bank had suspended.

The iron doors were swung to. A police guard arrived just as a terrific run ensued upon the depository.

Seney had once been worth seven millions. Now his fortune was irretrievably crippled. He was never active in business again.

Then hordes of harassed creditors could have been seen rushing for the doors of houses that were swept down by the banking troubles: Dyett & Company, a firm embarrassed by the Second National Bank defalcation; Donnell, Lawson & Company, whose downfall was attributed to the closing of the Metropolitan; O. M. Bogert, heavy dealers in puts and calls, in Broadway; Goffe & Randle, in New Street; Hotchkiss & Burnham and J. C. Williams, in Broad Street.

Under the rays of the cycle's dark star, one saw another unhappy youth fall to his ruin. The untried president of the Second National Bank, young John C. Eno, overconfident through the responsibilities thrust upon his immature shoulders, had become an unwitting instrument in the hands of the gamesters and intriguers with whom he had come into contact in Wall Street.

As he had been loaning out the banking funds entrusted to his care, the voracious riffraff of tricksters and beach combers which frequent the Street, and which had already jockeyed Ferdinand Ward, had filled the head of the credulous and temperamental youth with harebrained schemes. He suddenly awoke to reality. He had squandered the funds placed in his custody in unfruitful gambling operations.

When exposure came, Eno had already misappropriated some $4,000,000. Escaping a Federal warrant, he joined the rogues' colony in Canada. His father reimbursed the bank for the losses caused by his prodigal son's wild escapade.[1]

The cycle's caprice had also broken Matthew Morgan's Sons. In that old banking house in William Street, bluff old Henry Morgan, with his subconscious prejudice and dread of the perils of stock-gambling, found himself caught in the slump of Denver & Rio Grande. When the stock dropped to $7.25 a share, the old firm could not survive its loss of three millions.

While another string of houses was sliding into bankruptcy, W. B. Wheeler, a popular market operator, dashed suddenly into the offices of Hatch & Foote. He called loudly for Daniel B. Hatch, one

[1] Stedman: *N. Y. Stock Exchange.*

of the partners. "Come, Mr. Hatch," he exclaimed; "I deposited 5,000 shares of Erie here five minutes ago. Now the Fourth National won't certify your check!"

"There must be some mistake somewhere," protested Hatch, with a grave air of assurance. "Our check is perfectly good. I'll send a man to the bank with you and have it certified at once."

"No, you won't," yelled Wheeler. "You'll hand me back that Erie, and take your check."

Reluctantly, the broker then handed the certificates across his counter.

Wheeler departed smiling. To a group of his friends, who had just arrived on similar errands, he passed the observation: "Hatch & Foote are perfectly good. But I'll take no chances on a day like this."

On the Stock Exchange, a few moments later, the chairman read the suspension of Hatch & Foote. A long shout of surprise and dismay rose from the floor.

The house had been regarded as the soundest and most conservative in the city. Only two days before, Alfred S. Hatch, the junior member, had been elected president of the Exchange. He at once resigned from the post.[2]

But the brokers were becoming used to shocks and

[2] *Ibid.*

137

surprises. For days there had prevailed a delirium of panic on 'Change. Standard dividend-paying shares had fallen from a level already low. The rate for call money had run up so high as three per cent a day.

XVI

THE "SQUATTING" OF RUSSELL SAGE

ONE of the great enigmas of the crisis of '84 is that old Russell Sage should have been caught in its clutches.

That the necromancy of a psychic phenomenon should have influenced the hard headed money-lender, with his crafty, calculating mind, seems difficult of belief, but no other interpretation is available.

As an ex-Congressman, "Uncle Russell" had settled in Wall Street to divert his declining years by the sale of privileges. Now this is a highly technical business, and one which demands a keen sense of vision, and also the cool head of a trained speculator. Yet up to this year, Sage had never been proved wrong in his calculations.

Sage's office at this time was on the second floor of the "Arcade," on the southwest corner of Broadway and Rector Street.[1] He was then close upon seventy years. He looked the part of a simple country gentleman, with his slim side-whiskers, short, stubble beard, bland face and innocent-looking gray eyes.

[1] *Herald,* Dec. 5, 1891.

On that May-day of '84, when Seney's Metropolitan Bank suspended, a perturbed rumor sped through Wall Street that Uncle Russell, its oldest and most renowned dealer in "puts and calls," had squatted on his contracts. Mr. Sage began to face a small, private panic all his own. In essence, it was technical, and to the uninitiated it needs an explanation.

Notwithstanding an extraordinary capacity for anticipating the stock market, Mr. Sage had been selling "puts" freely on the rising market of the last few months. The sudden slump caused by the unexpected panic had upset all his calculations. Now a "put" entitles the purchaser to put or deliver stock to the seller, at a stipulated price, within a given time. In effect and practice, it is betting on the market movement of the stock selected.

Mr. Sage, for once, had bet on the losing side. Heretofore he had nearly always calculated aright, but now his frugal mind was dismayed by the dreadful amounts of cash money for which his customers were clamoring.

Uncle Russell had won for himself a serio-comic reputation for parsimony. He was the traditional skinflint of the Street.[2] The simple-minded but immensely shrewd old gentleman would probably

[2] Edward W. Bok: *Twice Thirty*, N. Y., 1925.

have been amazed at this misinterpretation of what to him was merely a habitual prudence.

Large amounts of stock had been delivered to Mr. Sage on his outstanding puts. At first he took and paid for them, but suddenly the payments stopped. The prudent old gentleman had availed himself of a stipulation printed on each of his puts, exacting 24 hours' previous notice that the stocks were to be offered to him. His outer office, meanwhile, was packed with brokers, customers and messengers, demanding checks for their proffered puts. But the checks were no longer forthcoming.

The panic still continuing on the following day, Mr. Sage's position became still more precarious, for the lower the quotations ran on stocks, the bigger became the losses on his puts. He then made access to his office more difficult. The doors were barred. Only those persons were admitted who had given him the requisite notice the day before.

Long lines of angry men and youths, waiting outside the closed doors, insisted that this was but a trick of the old privilege dealer to keep them standing there until after banking hours, and thus prevent them from cashing their puts the next day.

Third day in the run on Russell Sage's office.

The affair was serious.

Before nine o'clock, holders of privileges gathered

in front of the closed doors, all of them ready to present puts bearing Sage's promise to purchase stocks at prices far above those then prevailing in the market.

Half an hour later. Clamorous clients blocked the corridor and stairway. No longer a good-natured crowd. Ten o'clock passed. Office doors still barricaded.

It was evident that Uncle Russell calculated to profit in two ways by delaying payments. He was giving the stock market time to recuperate. Then he was diminishing his losses by frightening his put-holders into compromising their claims. Already alarmed persons were hawking Sage's puts about the Street, offering them at half their face value.[8]

Then the crowd attacked the three doors of the office and tried to break them down. The upper half of one door fell in with a crash. The imprisoned clerks sent for the police.

Men, waiting in the crowd, exchanged their experiences. Many had come to the offices two days before, for the stock market being so low, they were tempted to take the money that was due them. But they had been kept cooling their heels in the hall ever since. Now the market was recovering, and their profits were slipping away. They had already

[8] Stedman: *N. Y. Stock Exchange.*

142

lost thousands, because the clerks of the privilege dealer would not stamp their puts.

Finally Mr. Sage capitulated when the Stock Exchange threatened him with expulsion. He consented to admit his fellow brokers, but these, on emerging from his office, expressed their disgust at the manner in which the wily financier tried to compromise their claims.

One speculator, who held a put on Northwestern at 110, had the sum of $900 due him, since his stock was then selling at 101. Sage, however, refused to pay the full difference between the "put" price and the market price. He offered to compromise for $600. This was an example of nearly all the transactions.

Only about 60 per cent of the amounts actually due, were proffered by the obstinate old financier. A latent fear that he might be forced to suspend, induced the greater number of claimants to accept the sums offered.

On the succeeding day, Mr. Sage unbarred his doors. A partial truce was effected in the "put-'n'-call" warfare, but the financier persistently objected to paying face value on the puts presented.

Sunday then intervened. The old privilege dealer had a breathing spell.

In the end it was known that Mr. Sage had paid

143

out nearly $7,000,000 in cash since the Grant & Ward panic. The greater part of that sum was money which his clients had deposited with him, but a good two million dollars had been subtracted from his own bank balance. This proved a sad torment to his thrifty soul.

Indeed, some time after, Mr. Sage disappeared from his offices. He went into concealment. Nothing could be learned of his whereabouts. It was reported that his financial losses had wrecked his mind, that he had been placed in the care of an alienist, that his late ordeal had shattered his health.

And since, furthermore, it was known that Mr. Sage had not taken a vacation in forty years, he being vigorously opposed to that form of relaxation, many persons in Wall Street expected never to see him there again.

Meanwhile failures and defalcations occurred at intervals all through that summer of '84. The series wound up with the closing of the Wall Street Bank, in the Mills Building, due to the irregularities of its cashier. He had fled toward Canada, a defaulter.

During this period, the district saw its first invasion by "panic birds,"—white-haired old gentlemen, arriving in coaches and hacks to consult the officers of banks and trust companies regarding opportune investments. Portly in bearing, wearing swallow-tailed coats of ancient design, they could be seen having comfortable luncheons in quiet restaurant nooks. Their airs betokened perfect satisfaction with the unhappy conditions of the Street.

So ended the panic precipitated by the failure of Grant & Ward.

The Grants had lost their entire fortune. Rarely had a family been so thoroughly stripped of its all. Even the daily necessaries of life were actually wanting in their stricken home. The ruin was complete.

Buck had up to the last moment believed that he was worth $1,700,000. His brother, Jesse, had put borrowed money into the firm on the day previous to the failure.

The General had borne the shock with the fortitude of a soldier, although political enemies took advantage of his misfortunes even to impugn his honor; but secret grief soon afterward produced a fearful change in his appearance.

Grant turned over to Mr. Vanderbilt deeds to all his properties, including the Philadelphia dwelling given to him by residents of that city; his farm, even his personal trophies, and the cherished swords presented to him by citizens and soldiers. All this was in part payment for the $150,000 he had borrowed a few days before the failure; superb caskets, the gifts of cities through which he had traveled on his journey round the world,—curious and exquisite souvenirs from China and Japan. He spared nothing. Mr. Vanderbilt generously offered to return all these, with warm expressions of sympathy.

But Grant set to work on his memoirs to liquidate the debt. He forgot the terrible destruction of his hopes in re-living the scenes of his career,—he recaptured Fort Donaldson, again besieged Vicksburg, once more received the surrender at Appomattox, "fought all his battles o'er again." There came to him still another victory! The memoirs were finished, the debt was paid, even as the faltering pen dropped from his lifeless fingers.

A sheriff seized the home of Ferdinand Ward. The fugitive, pursued by detectives, was arrested, tried, convicted. When, a year later, his young wife first visited him in Sing Sing prison, where she saw him in convict's stripes, working as a stovemaker, hardened prison keepers could scarcely endure the sight of the young couple's heart-rending grief.

Ward served six and one-half years. His gull, old banker Fish, obtained a pardon after a four years' term.

XVII

GOLD shipments had been favorable. Grain crops had been good. Those reasons so confidently summed up by experts to explain the cyclical panic were conspicuous by their absence in the period preceding '84.

One's attention is riveted entirely upon the objectives and the characters of gamesters and fortune-hunters. Swept away by optimism, they exploited the future through unwarranted speculations.

Of such caliber were the two reckless youths, Ferdinand Ward and John C. Eno; of their type was that many-sided but unscrupulous genius, George I. Seney; poor, bedeviled old Henry Morgan, and cunning Russell Sage, caught in a web from which he wriggled out only by means of his able lack of conscience.

We see here, unquestionably, a duplication of the similarly concerted movement witnessed in the time prior to the panic of '57, when Robert Schuyler, head of the New Haven, his co-conspirator, Alexander Kyle, Jr., Paul, Belmont's cashier, and all those contrivers of lesser note, became defaulters, thieves and fugitives.

Present-day Wall Street assures us that such conditions no longer prevail. It tells us that the high moral plane of conduct now observed, the restrictions which surround the business of finance, make such practices impossible.

Conditions may have changed, it is true, but men have grown no better when called upon to face the storms of panic times. The deceptions, the hazards, the calamities of '57 and of '84, were duplicated in 1929.

The Princeton professor of to-day, who idealizes the Street,[1] the radical Western Senator, who regards it as the source of all evil, would seem both to be in error. As the most practical nation on earth, we appear to be singularly lacking in plain common sense in contemplating Wall Street, for there, business is strictly business. It is the philosophy of Wall Street's life to let the buyer beware, and the devil take the hindmost. It is needless to sit in judgment, to cite some moral law, or quote the Golden Rule. In the stern facts that face finance, the human equation can never be removed, and conditions must always arise in the life of communities, when men

[1] See Joseph Stagg Lawrence: *Wall Street and Washington*, Princeton University Press, 1929.

sweep aside all barriers with which civilization and morality have surrounded them.

We are observing panics, looking for a common derivation of these social convulsions. We begin to perceive that the panic is produced invariably by groups of men, acting individually, yet in concert, who undergo the various phases of the classic cycle: the promotion of some great enterprise, the execution of a headstrong speculation, an initial success, carried to extremes, a check, and sudden failure.

In this account of the unhappy year of '84, it is a relief to conclude it with a cheering episode.

Wall Street awoke one day to learn with gratitude that its concern about that unique character, without whom our financial history is incomplete,— namely Uncle Russell Sage—had been quite needless.

Despite the rumors of the old money-lender's miserable fate, he was discovered recuperating in the small village of Quogue, L. I. During his disappearance, he had been living there quite happily. He was soon drawn back to the Street by the necessity for attending directorate meetings of the thirty or forty corporations in which he was interested. He was never absent from such occasions, the incentive being the ten dollar gold piece which each director is entitled to receive.

On his return, the old privilege dealer expounded his peculiar philosophy of life, as he had experienced it in the crisis. "My goodness, the way I was abused was shameful," he complained. "Just imagine! I am the originator of the privilege business. I began it twenty years ago, just to accommodate small traders in stocks who hadn't enough money to put up a margin in a broker's hands. And dear me, what a blessing it has proved to Wall Street! I never made a cent out of my privileges. I sold them only for the good of the Street. Now they turn around and abuse me outrageously. The idea! But you know, we must forgive a great deal in this world, and make allowances for a great deal more."

Mr. Sage continued for years thereafter to harvest ten dollar gold pieces at board meetings. He resumed his vocation of selling puts, calls and straddles to eager speculators. He never made another miscalculation in the stock market. He never "broke." He lived plainly and abstemiously unto the patriarchal age of four-score and ten. For the race is not always to the swift, nor is the battle to the man with scruples.

VI

THE TRUST LUNACIES

XVIII

ANOTHER cycle spun its enchanted course after the panic of '84.

It brought a new world into being. It hummed with industrial life. It was filled with innovations. Fresh enterprises were fomented into tremendous expansions.

Under the spell of this orbit, an army of ingenious gentlemen was prevailed upon to attempt to create monopolies in the innumerable industries that had sprung to life in cities, towns and countrysides.

The list of these enterprises confuses the imagination with its numbers.

One encountered schemes to monopolize the production of beer, bluestone and chemicals; sewer pipe, coke, copper, fruits, gas, guns, hides, linseed oil, lumber, matches, nails, paper, peanuts, rice, rubber, salt, school slates, silks, soaps, storage warehouses and sugar.

The Whiskey Trust, under the title of the Distillers' & Cattle Feeders' Company, had been preceded by the Cottonseed Oil Trust; but the most popular combinations were the lead, sugar, pig iron and cattle trusts.

In describing the industrial mergers and combinations of 1929, a Yale economist dubbed them an invention of the present day, designed for economy of operation and scientific management.

But really, now, these combines were devised by the men of the early nineties under the pretext of saving operating costs. The term "scientific management" had not then been coined.

In this movement, engineered in the days of our fathers, trusts of stock were in actuality created as a means of stifling competition, even as they were in 1929. Business men are not altruists: nobody expects them to be. The human thought is that when all possible rivals are combined into one corporation, the logical conclusion is to raise prices to artificial levels and keep them there.

This attempt, made in the early nineties of the nineteenth century, was copied in the late twenties of the twentieth century.

On the floodtide of industrialism, two opportunists advanced, bending their destinies to circumstances and winning the unenviable fame of having precipitated the panic of 1893.

The first of these, A. A. McLeod, president of the Philadelphia & Reading Railroad, fostered a conception as daring and brilliant as any of those dreamed by the industrial promoters; this was to monopolize the output of anthracite; then to advance the price of black diamonds.

Wall Street's most powerful bankers at first applauded McLeod's decision and encouraged his delusion. With their aid, he arranged leases of the Lehigh Valley and Jersey Central roads, gained control of the Lackawanna's coal business and bought the New York & New England Railroad.[1]

The second of these adventurers attained an even more spectacular success. The Cordage Trust was the offspring of the brain of James M. Waterbury. He established a reputation for turning binding twine into gold with a whisk of his pen.

Waterbury's father had left him three millions. When the father of E. Berry Wall, who had headed the second largest concern in the cordage business, died, and the Wall estate joined with the Waterburys, the National Cordage Company was founded.

One by one, smaller plants were purchased, in Boston, New Bedford and elsewhere. But possession of the plant of one John Good was the supreme object to be desired. His works were valued at two millions. But it seemed impossible to make a deal

[1] Stedman: *N. Y. Stock Exchange.*

with him. Like the Trojan warrior, Good lay sulking in his tent.

By May, 1891, the Cordage Trust, although capitalized at fifteen millions, had been able to harry only 40 per cent of the trade into its combination. Thus 60 per cent of the rope manufacturers of the country showed themselves opposed to the projected monopoly. The men in the combine found that it was not so easy, after all, to fetter the trade. Then they deliberately reduced the price of the product of their spindles. This was done to force the outsiders to join them. So the trust was enabled to buy up fifteen more companies, through quiet purchases; but it concealed the fact that it was losing money.

Talented promotion was triumphant in the end. Waterbury made a rather expensive arrangement with his most vigorous rival, the reluctant John Good. He agreed to pay the other a bonus of $200,000 cash a year for keeping his manila rope mills shut; then he took an option at seven millions on Good's two-million-dollar plant.

Meanwhile, an avalanche of securities, issued by the industrial trusts to effect their mergers, was piling up in banking houses. This paper was held there as collateral for call loans. The bankers had also thus committed themselves to the program of business combinations.

The brokers, of course, were involved up to their necks. Among those who had plunged into the trust madness was the Hon. Stephen White, the noted "Deacon" of Plymouth Church. A bold, dashing stock operator, this. He had been a spectacular figure in the Street for two generations. His first great deal had been in Lackawanna, in '84. He had manipulated the shares of that fine old property so adroitly, that he had increased the fortunes, so it was said, of half the members of Plymouth Church; later he had met with financial mishaps. But at this period he was operating the shares of the Whiskey Trust, and so successfully that, on the first of November, '92, he was already rated at two millions.

In the meantime, James M. Waterbury was displaying his finesse. He issued ten millions in Cordage Trust common stock. He sold it on the market at $70 a share. Then he engaged the services of James R. Keene, the veteran stock manipulator, to create a pool.

In Keene's hands, and under his expert supervision, Cordage began its advance. Eventually it commanded the price of $140 a share. That put it next in value to such standard securities as New York Central and Manhattan Railway. It sold even above Western Union.

As McLeod had reserved the benefits of his an-

thracite promotion to his banker friends, so Waterbury had no intention of permitting the rabble rout
to enjoy the proceeds from his new system of progress. The profits were to be distributed only to
members of his own class, for he calculated that social
influence would prove an element leading to much
higher success.

Waterbury developed this ambition in his country
home. This was a fine place in Westchester County,
near Pelham, which adjoined the Country Club.
There, in those days of happy anticipations, one witnessed the leader of industrial finance displaying his
talents as a social leader. He drew about him persons
with similar sympathies and aspirations.

House parties. Yachting parties. The celebrated
society circus. The guests, in ringside attire, exhibiting themselves as bareback riders, acrobats, clowns
and sword swallowers. Youth and beauty were added
lures to the entertainment. Dinner was served in a
sawdust-floored tent. Balloons floated in midair.
Pennants waved from the canvas top.

Young folk, born to riches, were represented in
plentiful numbers in the membership of the Country
Club. All these were to become stock-holders in
Cordage. In this their spiritual guides were Henry
Allen, the Kentuckian, a broker who had joined the
stock campaign in Whiskey Trust shares, Schuyler

Walden, also a member of the Stock Exchange, and E. Berry Wall, the noted Beau Brummell of the happy set.[2]

All these folk regarded Waterbury as their great benefactor. For were not the fruits of his Cordage Trust enterprise reserved exclusively for them—the socially elect?

When Keene had put the stock up to $140, Waterbury doubled the fortunes of his friends by paying a scrip dividend of ten millions in common shares. The Country Club palpitated with delight over this sudden act of beneficence.[3]

There was a wild scramble on the part of other favored mortals, who were regarded as eligible, to win entrance to the promoter's charmed circle.

And so the occult cycle, weaving its beautiful but faithless spells, had furtively entrapped the votaries in the meshes of its net.

[2] *N. Y. World*, May 5, 1893.
[3] *Herald*, May 6, 1893.

XIX

THE PANIC OF '93

THUS arrived the early months of 1893.

An atmosphere heavily charged with mystery. Money had been drained from Wall Street for working supposed tin mines in South Dakota, and for buying Florida lands. The latter were to be unloaded upon foreigners as future sugar plantations.

Distorted visions preceded an approaching cataclysm, as in '37, as in the years tending toward 1929. Venturers caused new towns to spring to life all over the South. These communities were dowered in the imaginations of their contrivers with infinite possibilities; but they proved themselves bottomless pits for Northern capital.

After the passage of some thirteen months, one sees James M. Waterbury, absorbed by the cares, the prodigious perils of his mighty adventure, asking himself a question: What had brought his apparently successful Cordage scheme to a sudden stop?

In truth, it was a sequence of events which were beyond the control of its promoter.

Waterbury had advanced his stock to $140. He

160

had distributed a ten-million-dollar-share disbursement. He was paying dividends of 12 per cent. Yet in the face of this apparent affluence, the Wall Street banks had become wary of loaning their money on Cordage collateral. The bankers suspected something.

The chief competitor of the Trust, John Good, had reopened his plant. Once more he was producing rope. He justified himself with the reproach that the agreement to pay him $200,000 a year, so long as he refrained from manufacturing, had been broken. This development had already caused the Trust a loss of $7,000,000.[1]

Waterbury needed money now. He had begun endorsing notes. Lately he had become involved quite deeply in such transactions; in his need, he finally authorized an issue of preferred stock, but the Exchange brokers, grown fearful of his stock-jobbing scheme, refused to take the shares.

The failure of the new issue caused Cordage common to drop from its price of $140 to $70. Then the favored stockholders of the Country Club, whose wealth had been doubled by the scrip dividend, suddenly found to their dismay that *they were no richer than they had been before!* [2]

[1] *World*, May 5, 1893.   [2] *Herald*, May 6, 1893.

161

Late on a May evening in '93, the first shadow of catastrophe fell.

The cheerful spirits of a gathering in the Country Club were plunged into consternation. News came that a receiver had unexpectedly been appointed for the Cordage Trust that night.

The company had found itself unable to meet a bank's call for a miserable $50,000. All were thunderstruck. The crisis at once threatened to bankrupt many of Waterbury's friends.

The next morning, a dismal rain. It beat against the windows of the National Cordage Company's building in Front Street. Still more disheartening were the scenes in the interior of the expensively equipped offices.[8]

A sorry group of fashionable young men had hurried down here from their Westchester club. They were eager to investigate the truth of the announcement, learned overnight, at once unexpected, incredible, dismaying, that Cordage had gone to smash. Overcoats buttoned up to their chins, to hide the betraying fact that they had not been in bed all night, yet traces of sleepless vigil were portrayed on their pale, lined faces.

Sackcloth and ashes had overwhelmed the friends of Schuyler Walden, of Berry Wall, the magnificent,

[8] *Herald*, May 6, 1893.

162

of the great James M. Waterbury, himself,—of all those who had been entertained at the latter's countryplace near Pelham. They had been his guests on yachting parties, and had taken parts in the Country Club circus some years before. Now their dejection, their grief, made them objects of compassion even to the cluster of sharp-featured brokers who were lingering in the outer office.[4]

The young men were anxious to interview their friend, Waterbury, to learn what fragments of their fortunes they could salvage in the big disaster. But their onetime benefactor was busied in conferences behind the locked doors of the board room, and remained inaccessible.

The dazed and disheartened young members of the Westchester Country Club then wandered disconsolately down to the financial district. There they witnessed scenes which were symptomatic of the cyclical drama.

In the enormous crowds that filled Broad Street, there passed from lip to lip, news of the downfall of the great Cordage pool. Keene, who had been its manipulator, was accused of having been the first to get out from under. He had left his associates to bear the loss. The Cordage crowd had tried to un-

[4] *Ibid.*

load upon the public something that had rolled back and crushed them.[5]

At the Stock Exchange entrance, "Charley" Deacon, veteran doorkeeper, struggled to keep the passageway open. Visitors streamed up to the gallery. There, under the gorgeous ceiling, they peered down upon a wild spectacle.

In the Cordage Trust circle, hats were being smashed, coats torn, cravats ruined. Here was an agony that meant financial life or death to many. Cordage common had gone off 18 points. The preferred had lost 22. Suddenly howls went up from the floor. Those who could distinguish the words, heard the ominous cry: "Nineteen for Cordage!"[6]

The shares, a few moments later, went down to $12.

Distracted, thirsting for counsel, the youths of the Country Club sought out their friend, Berry Wall. They knew that he had a desk in the offices of Allen & Company, where he was supposed to represent the Cordage interests, but they found that Allen & Company had failed.

Not long before, two operators, speculating in this office, had divided a quarter of a million made out of ventures in Whiskey and Sugar. Then they had turned to Cordage, and all the money had been lost.

[5] *Herald*, May 6, 1893.   [6] *Ibid.*

164

In fact, the Cordage pool, working in part through Allen's office, were now his debtors for heavy sums. He had been carrying more than 40,000 shares for them at 60. With the drop had come a loss of more than $2,000,000, with no one to meet it.

Then Waterbury's followers made for the offices of Schuyler Walden. Again disaster. He, too, had suspended. Walden lamented that in twenty-five years of Wall Street experience, he had never seen anything like this. He had waited for promised aid. None had come. He had appealed to Mr. Waterbury. The latter told him he had not a dollar left in the world.

Walden had carried Cordage for his customers even after their margins had been eaten up. B. L. Smyth & Company, also identified with the Trust, had gone under.

Thus ended the illusions of the victims of the pool.

The Cordage crash seemed some occult signal for the halting of enterprise. All those opportunist combinations, intended to restrain trade, began to falter. Receiverships engulfed them. Plants closed. The monopolies that had multiplied and expanded in the heart of the landscape, one by one exploded, fell to the ground, bestrewed it with their wreckage.

Persons who had fancied themselves in possession of secure incomes, discovered that investments which they had considered safest, ceased to pay them dividends.

The shrinkage in money values had its immediate repercussion upon the banks. The National Bank of Deposit, in Broadway, closed its doors, as did the Canal Street Bank. The Madison Square Bank liquidated its affairs, the St. Nicholas Bank refusing to act longer as its clearing agent. Then the St. Nicholas closed in its turn. The Equitable Mortgage Company, which had done an annual business of three millions, and the Jarvis-Conklin Mortgage Trust Company, with a capital of nearly four millions, went into receiverships.

Now banks began failing all over the country. Twenty-five National depositories suspended in June. Seventy-eight in July. Thirty-eight in August.

Able Wall Street houses, which had weathered countless other storms, went under. Horace L. Hotchkiss & Company failed. Then came the crash of H. I. Nicholas & Company, followed by that of John B. Dumont. All these had been unable to sustain margins for loans.

For several nights, lights had been observed burning brightly in the Wall Street offices of the Hon. Stephen V. White, the noted "Deacon," after the Street itself had long been darkened. Clerks were casting up accounts there, to learn how matters stood.

166

In the end, announcement of the Deacon's suspension. It was the fourth one in his long career. The first had come in 1868. Another arrived in 1872. That was followed by one in 1891.

Heretofore, the popular Deacon had always settled his accounts in full, but he had met a fearful loss in the fall of Whiskey Trust shares. Then, on the day when Cordage broke, the terrific drop in the market had used up his fortune of two millions.

And still the Deacon was unconquered. In some way he compromised with his creditors. He resumed his seat on 'Change. Ten years later he sold it, retiring with honors from the Street at the ripe age of seventy.

XX

CONCEALED beneath episodes and events, the industrial boom had been silently encouraged by currency inflation.

The Sherman Silver Purchase Act of 1890 had compelled purchase of heavy amounts of white metal. This was paid for by Treasury notes, redeemable in gold.

Yellow metal went out of the country as new notes were pumped into circulation.

Its wealth was being siphoned out of the National Treasury.

Money trouble was the manifest peculiarity of the long-drawn-out panic of '93. Depositors crowded counting-rooms of savings banks, begging for their lodgments. Drained and frightened banks exercised their lawful privilege in withholding payment. The Clearing House protected depositories by issuing loan certificates. Deposit institutions limited the amounts of currency they consented to pay on presented drafts.

Merchants and manufacturers were forced to the wall in thousands.

Multitudes of unemployed were swelled in numbers by every failure.

Hungry workmen rioted in the streets of New York and Chicago.

The formidable list of bankruptcies grew like a mortuary roll in times of plague.

Ready money became shockingly scarce. Gold was still sweeping out of the country. Payments of wages by certified check was a new experience for many folk who had never before handled bank checks. These were issued by business houses, corporations and contractors. They were in amounts of two, five and ten dollars. One saw salaried workers passing them in drinking places and restaurants. There the cashiers were driven to desperate expedients in order to make change.

Government statements asserted that there was $17,000,000 in more money of all kinds circulating in the country than the month before; but frightened folk began to hoard their dollars. A new and curious traffic developed. Money in small denominations was dealt in at a premium in Wall Street.

In many dingy little ground-floor offices in the Street, one saw lines of men, bearing satchels or suitcases. They were posted before long counters, where they bargained for ready cash. Stacked up behind brass screens were small bundles of one, two, five or ten-dollar bills. Some were made up of twenty-dollar notes, fewer still of fifties. Most of this currency was worn, crumpled, dirty. That testified to its long circulation. Beside such bundles were heaped gold pieces and a fair supply of silver cartwheels.

The traffickers behind the counters would sweep heaps of notes and piles of coin into bags, and shove the lots over to the purchasers, just as grocers might hand over bars of soap or cartons of sugar. Most of the buyers seemed to be in pairs. While one man stowed away notes and coin in his satchel or canvas bag, his companion would withdraw to an end of the counter and draw a check in settlement.

Were the purchase a small one, say of $1,000 in current money, the buyer made out his draft for $1,020. In other words, the country's currency was being sold in these dingy shops at two per cent more than its face value.

It was calculated that $15,000,000 in current money was thus traded in Wall Street during the crisis.

These conditions tempted bear speculators to depress prices. To themselves, no doubt, they justified their methods. By others they were regarded as more clever than scrupulous.

There was, for example, the ruse concerted by a stockbroker who had earned for himself the title of

"Plunger." He was credited with making heavy sums on the short side of the market in spectacular ways. One day, in the bond group on the floor of the Exchange, the "Plunger" offered to sell $50,000 in Government Fours at 110¾ "payable in currency." The market at the moment was a full point above that price, and this tempted the representative of a banking house to buy the lot under the condition specified, although the cash stipulation was entirely unprecedented.

The Plunger appeared at the offices of the banking house next morning with his bonds, and asked for the currency.

"I have it all ready for you," replied the banker. He led the bear operator into an inner room. There a table was spread high with five and ten dollar gold pieces. The amount—more than $55,000—made a considerable heap. It weighed upwards of 200 pounds.

Now, perhaps, the bear operator had thought to entrap the banker. Knowing the difficulty then experienced in obtaining legal tender notes, he had sold the bonds "payable in currency," not reckoning gold as such. But he had reasoned that the buyer could not pay in paper money. Had that been the case, a despatch to London, stating that U. S. bonds could not be sold for currency, would have made a dramatic bear argument.

So the broker at once resented what he regarded as the banker's trick. He exclaimed that the yellow metal was not currency. He refused to accept it, and would not deliver the bonds.

The banker, who, no doubt, was chuckling inwardly, insisted, nevertheless, that United States gold coin was the best currency in the world.

But the Plunger refused to accept the tender.

The banker, thereupon, threatened to resort to a rule of the Stock Exchange. He informed the other that if he did not accept the gold and deliver the bonds by quarter past two o'clock, the securities would be bought in for his account "under the rule." This would have been tantamount to announcing the broker's suspension.

But the speculator, still feeling himself in the right, departed from the banking house in wrath.

Who can account for the illogicalities in human conduct?

The bear returned later, however, and renewed his demand for "paper currency." This was refused, the gold coin was once more tendered, but again declined.

The banker then reminded the Plunger that he had no right, in law, to discriminate against any class of the circulating medium of the country. But the broker left again, still obsessed by his own viewpoint. He amended his attitude before the arrival of the fatal hour that had been specified. Shortly after one o'clock, he drew up before the banker's offices in a carriage, accompanied by two men. The 200-pounds' weight of gold was carried out, stacked in the carriage and carted away.

Wall Street, despite the gloom which hung upon it, extracted merriment from this episode, and the manner in which the banker had outwitted the speculative broker.[1]

But the incident rankled in the Plunger's mind. He still clung to his aggressive point of view. He had a large credit balance with the Bank of the Manhattan Company, so he presented a check there for $50,000, requesting payment in notes.

The bank refused to surrender that amount of currency. After a discussion, the bear reduced his demand to $25,000, which sum he received in paper money. The bank then requested him to take up his account, and he did so, transferring it to another institution.[2]

These disagreeable experiences still possessing his mind, the indiscreet bear, caught in an argument on the floor of the Exchange, exclaimed to a fellow

---

[1] *Herald,* July 20, 1893.　　[2] *Ibid.*

173

broker: "The Manhattan Company couldn't pay me in cash!"

Surrounding brokers, who overheard the remark, set up a howl of condemnation at what they considered unjustifiable bear tactics.

The unfortunate Plunger was then suspended from the privileges of the Exchange for one year by the Board of Governors, owing to his ill-advised observation.

XXI

ALARMED by the flight of gold, the Senators in Washington debated annulment of the Sherman Act.

The silver purchase bill was repealed. Its end was registered by the signature of President Cleveland on November 1.

But the repeal had been so retarded, that the *coup de grâce* to this year of waste and disorganization could not be averted from the vulnerable world of the railroads.

It will be recalled that A. A. McLeod, the Reading's president, imitating the methods of his industrial brethren, had built up a brilliant anthracite coal monopoly. This he had done by combining the coal carriers, the Reading, the Lehigh, the Jersey Central, the Lackawanna; and he had purchased the New York & New England railway.

McLeod had engineered his deal through means of a pool in Reading shares. The pool had hypothecated its Reading stocks with friendly bankers, who at first approved the scheme. In this wise he had borrowed the money with which to carry the New England share holdings.

But with the first lowering clouds of the cyclical thunderstorm, that portion of New England stock still remaining in the market, became lamentably weak. The bankers, now alarmed, began to call in their loans. McLeod's pool was compelled to sacrifice its holdings in the two railroad companies. Terrific masses of Reading and New England securities were hurled out upon the stock market.[1]

Thus succumbed the big anthracite coal combination.

A receiver was named for the Reading.

Railway earnings fell off in extraordinary fashion. There came the third downfall of the Erie road. It announced its inability to pay off maturing loans. The ill-starred Northern Pacific, origin of so many previous heartbreaks, once more was in trouble. It disclosed a floating debt of nine millions, and was pronounced bankrupt. Receivers were then appointed successively for the Atchison, the Union Pacific and the New York & New England railroad systems.[2]

In asking oneself the cause of the panic of '93, the

[1] Stedman: *N. Y. Stock Exchange.*
[2] *Chronicle*, Feb. 25, July 26, Dec. 23, Dec. 27, 1893.

answer seems self-evident: it lay in the terrific fer-
ment of promotions in the early nineties.

The blame must be laid primarily upon McLeod
and the bankers who encouraged his anthracite monopoly, and upon Waterbury and the group of high
gamblers who surrounded him in the Cordage combination.

The downfall of Cordage had merely accelerated
the ball that had started rolling after the breakdown
of the coal monopoly. Against this troubled background loomed the operation of the Sherman Silver
Purchase Act. With the final proof of the insub-
stantiality of the industrial combinations, the year had
ended in the flight of money.

To the people of that time, the Free Silver scare
was a bogey that obscured their vision. They attributed all their troubles to this concrete issue, but panic
would have come without the silver problem.

In 1893, a merger of binder twine plants into the
Cordage combine; monopolies in anthracite coal, in
whiskey distilleries; a rage for trusts in sugar, cottonseed oil, lead, pig iron, cattle, rice, rubber, soap
and peanuts,—trusts unlimited.

In 1929, a similar mania for mergers; combinations
of motion picture theaters, radio companies, steel,
utilities and natural gas-pipe lines; chains of banks,
chains of groceries, chains of drug stores, airy air-

plane ventures, all-too-optimistic investment trusts.

Not the shadow of difference between these two periods. They display the same beginnings and the same endings.

Yes, and the same widespread consequences. Nobody spared. The panic's hand felt by the laborer in the street, the mechanic in the shop; by the retired capitalist, the tenement dweller, the rich man's family.

In 1929 came the crop of college economists. Their useful labors and virtuous intentions no one would deny. They were apostles of a new inductive and experimental school. They taught us facts of the new era. It heralded an increased "tempo" or acceleration in the formation of mergers. It had discovered that these made for lower production costs. Science for the first time applied to industry. Economies bringing larger values for common stocks. And these greater values were to remain—they were established on a permanently higher plateau.

The same arguments, the same logic, the same theories.

And the country was gulled in '93, as the world was bamboozled in '29.

Wall Street moves forward always. That is a truism. We have been observing its progress by the records of its catastrophes. But our confident proponents of the new era thoughtlessly made themselves apologists for the illustrious jazz financiers of '29. Their teachings, so far, have proved that they have learned nothing, invented nothing and discovered nothing.

In the human scope of the panic, one constantly sees its leaders subject to similar limitations of judgment, of misdirected energies, often of rogueries. But it is through the efforts of such men that the wheels of the cyclical phenomenon are set in motion.

And from out of all this there emerges a queer but inescapable conclusion: in every cycle there appear to be forces at work which prevent practical and experienced men from realizing the inevitable outcome of their promotions and underwritings.

Why do they all engage in these activities at a similar time and in a similar way? Ah, there we are faced with another problem. We are still on our journey toward something yet unexplained, something we may yet discover, something yet to be disclosed.

VII

THE MERGER MANIAS

XXII

MEN OF THE TWENTIETH CENTURY

IN the panic of 1901, four men were its conscious instruments. Perhaps one man only, for he, with his imposing style, his sense of vigorous life, compelled his personality to stand out and overshadow the entire group.

J. Pierpont Morgan at this period was about 65 years old. His mustache was black and full. His hair was white. His eyes were small and glazed. His nose large, reddish and bulbous.

But these defects in appearance were all subordinated to Morgan's commanding presence. He was large and tall, with a masterful manner. His bulky figure was generally clothed in a black frock coat and gray trousers. He flourished a yellow cane. In his cravat was pinned the famous black pearl.

Morgan had first arrived in Wall Street in the panic of '57, from his father's London banking house. For a long time he was hardly known beyond his own moneyed circle. Only in the last fifteen years had he developed his mastery of the Street. Even now, scarcely fifty men in Wall Street had a speaking ac-

183

quaintance with this proud, exclusive and nearly always silent banker.[1]

Eight years had elapsed since the panic of '93 had exploded the artificial monopolies. But from the ashes of these failures, there now emerged yet larger combinations. More permanent, more lasting. Prosperity had led to rapid accumulations of capital.

In the speculations of 1901, John W. Gates assumed the headship of a group of financiers who became conspicuous experts in promotions. Morgan, then captain of a far superior group of capitalists, formed his Steel Trust, the greatest Morgan enterprise, and his most lasting achievement. He engaged that veteran manipulator, James R. Keene, who had worked the pool in the evil-omened Cordage Trust shares, to market Steel Common. Keene managed the flotation with marked ability. Morgan followed this promotion by financing the International Mercantile Marine, and the Harvester Trust.

The public had now a conception of Morgan as a man of granite, ruthless, perhaps, but often magnanimous, and gifted at all times with terrible energies. The glamor of his name had never reached such greatness. People felt for him, not popularity, to be sure, but tremendous admiration and a sort of awe.

[1] Carl Hovey: *The Life Story of J. Pierpont Morgan*, N. Y., 1912.

The second member of this unforgettable quartette had a great domed head. Below middle height, he was muscular and even leonine. Hairs of a short, ragged beard half concealed the expression of his full lips. The flight of an arrow, in his boyhood days, had robbed this Northwestern pioneer of the sight of one eye; but the immense eye that remained could look into a listener, and down and through him, for James Jerome Hill had the hypnotic power.

This tremendous man always frightened Wall Street with his railroad calculations. "Low costs of operation!" How his majestic phrase and his compelling figures alarmed the railway financiers. But they professed to ridicule the theories they secretly feared.

The inspiration to build the pioneer railroad of the Northwest came to Hill on his observing how rank the grass grew where gophers and the wheels of the Red River carts had loosened the upturned soil. He bought the St. Paul & Pacific from its Amsterdam owners, and built it up into the Great Northern System across the Cascade Mountains to the Pacific.[2]

Just as Hill's Great Northern reached the Pacific and its beckoning trade of the Orient, the Northern Pacific, as we saw, fell once more into bankruptcy in '93. The building of the one road had been as unwise

[2] Joseph Gilpin Pyle: *Life of James J. Hill*, 1917.

as that of the other had been prudent. Then Hill, and his banker, Morgan, set to work to reorganize the Northern Pacific. They had bought a heavy stock interest in it. Its strategy was of deep importance to the Great Northern.

For the Union Pacific, under the management of Edward H. Harriman, was stealthily trying to get control of the Northern Pacific and the Burlington. Hill's comprehensive glance saw his rival planning to command the entire West, from Mexico to the Northwest. He saw himself threatened with being closed up in the narrow territory between his rails and the Canadian border, shut out from Nebraska, Kansas, Missouri, South Dakota, Iowa, Illinois and Wisconsin.[3]

It had been a trying uphill climb for the pioneer of the Northwest country. What a scramble it had been in the early years to raise money to buy the St. Paul & Pacific bonds; then building a line through an Indian country and across the mountains; close figuring on rates; supplying his farmers with highgrade stock.

The year of 1901 had come, big with destiny for Hill. A hawk-eyed little stockbroker, weak of body but fierce in will, bred in Wall Street and trained in its devious ways, had started out to wrest from the

[3] Pyle: *Life of J. J. Hill.*

186

fangs and claws of this grizzled old mountain lion the fruits of his struggles for the last twenty-eight years.[4]

At least he had been a stockbroker,—the third member of the group that set the conjuncture of 1901 in motion. In his boyhood, as a little padshover, bullied by brokers' clerks, he had carried stock quotations from office to office before the appearance of the stock ticker in Wall Street. Those days were long past now, of course. At this period he was a financier, controlling an extensive railway domain.[5]

In manner, Harriman was brusque, almost to rudeness. Because, perhaps, of some reaction from his tyrannized boyhood, or maybe by reason of the physical pain that racked his slight body; or through the burden of multitudes of matters constantly weighing upon him, the need for every minute of his time, and a blind hatred for irksome detail.[6]

Harriman had linked the Union Pacific to the Southern Pacific. With the Morgan Line of steamers, he had made it a continuous transportation system from New York to San Francisco; but the railroad monopoly of the Southwest was not enough for him.

Harriman, now so often on a sick bed, cringed with unhappiness. That rugged old pioneer of the Indian

[4] *Ibid.*
[5] George Kennan: *E. H. Harriman*, 1922.
[6] *Ibid.*

country—James Jerome Hill—stood in his light. Hill was his rival in the trade of the Orient—and Harriman could brook no rival.

And Harriman realized that Hill was strong. Morgan was Hill's financier; Hill was backed by the fortunes of several aged Canadian Pacific men who had followed their old friend in his Great Northern adventure.

With his Union and Southern Pacifics, Harriman ruled the Southwest. Hill commanded the Northwest with his Great Northern and his control of the Northern Pacific.

But neither of these men had an outlet to Chicago for his railway lines.

Now the Burlington provided a roadway to Chicago.

Harriman and his banker, Jacob H. Schiff, of Kuhn, Loeb & Company, suddenly decided to buy control of the Burlington, because in doing this they would score a tremendous advantage over their rival.

Swiftly and secretly the two financiers began buying Burlington shares. They had accumulated about nine millions of the securities, when they were abruptly confronted by a disturbing fact.

Somebody else had already swept the market clean of the rest of Burlington stock!

Schiff and Harriman's sensibilities were then outraged by a report that it was Hill who had been the sly purchaser.

The prudent Schiff who, by the way, was the fourth principal to play his part in the affairs of 1901, had come to Wall Street from Germany in 1865. He had had intimate financial contacts with "Jim" Hill for the last fifteen years.[7]

It was but in obedience to a natural impulse that Schiff, taking his partner, Harriman, with him, should visit the old Northwestern pioneer, and ask him bluntly whether it was true that he was buying Burlington.

Then Hill, pursing up his full lips, and opening his amazing eye, assured both men solemnly that, neither directly nor indirectly, was he interested in Burlington. He had no intention whatever of controlling that property.[8]

Mr. Schiff is on record as saying that he accepted this statement. He could not believe that a man with whom he had been associated for fifteen years, and whom he believed to be his friend, would willingly deceive him.[9]

Yet sad to relate, to Schiff's distress and Harriman's rage, they soon after found out the reason for

[7] Dr. Cyrus Adler: *Jacob H. Schiff, His Life and Letters.*
[8] *Ibid.*
[9] *Ibid.*

the absence of Burlington shares in the market. Hill and Morgan had bought the road, under their very noses. Those two gentlemen had spent more than two hundred million dollars. They had split up control of Burlington between Great Northern and Northern Pacific. It was they who now controlled the route to Chicago.[10]

Schiff's offices were then at No. 7 Pine Street. He induced Hill to visit him there. Making no concealment of his wounded feelings, he taxed the railroad pioneer with his deception.

Then old "Jim" Hill made a confession. He had been sorry, he said, to have had to mislead his good friend, but owing to Schiff's relations with the Union Pacific, a rival road, he had felt compelled to do so. Furthermore, he added, he felt deep distrust for the man whom Schiff had brought with him on that previous interview, namely, the "Little Wizard of Wall Street." Hill would have ruined his own plans by revealing his hand to the enemy—Harriman.[11] And so his had been the lie of expediency, which was quite justified by the code of Wall Street.

Hill's confession further fired Harriman's resentment. The old Pine Street banker tried to still the rage of his little financial partner. He promised to

[10] Stedman: *N. Y. Stock Exchange.*
[11] See Adler: *Jacob H. Schiff.*

see what he could accomplish by diplomacy, that being his favorite weapon. Schiff tried to strike a bargain with Morgan and Hill. He asked to be permitted to share in Burlington control. The two successful rivals turned deaf ears to his pleas.

For days thereafter, Harriman haunted the banking house in Pine Street. There they sat conferring: the man with the dark, penetrating eyes, gnawing the mustache that fell heavily over his lips, and the quiet, sedate old banker.

Harriman chafed, fumed. He dwelt on the evil consequences to Union Pacific, following from a consolidation of the Great Northern, Northern Pacific and Burlington, under the skillful management of their old rival in St. Paul, with his deadly theories of low operating costs.

Schiff advised temporizing-diplomacy. But temporizing had failed, fretted Harriman. They must play some bold stroke, he argued,—the most audacious ever made in the American railway world.

Schiff abhorred strife and battle; it interrupted the making of money; but the resourceful mind of the stockbroker won over the caution of the banker.

Harriman had discovered a vulnerable link in the armor of their enemies. Morgan and Hill professed to own Northern Pacific:—yes, but it was merely nominal control, through possession of a minority interest. Actual ownership still lay in the stock market and in the outright investments held by individuals in the United States and Europe.

It was still in Schiff and Harriman's power to obtain a proper protection for their Union Pacific against eventual disaster. They could yet gain that voice in the Great Northern–Northern Pacific–Burlington situation, which friendly appeals had failed to obtain.

They would set quietly to work to accumulate Northern Pacific stock. But not with a view, so Schiff cautioned his partner, of actually taking away management of the property from those in whose possession it was. No, but solely to exercise a politic influence upon that management.

Harriman professed to agree, but he smiled inwardly at the suggestion that he should rely upon the magnanimity of his antagonists. He read them better.

However, the two men now sold their Burlington stock. They set about accumulating more than sixty millions in Northern Pacific in the markets of the United States and Europe.

They would get absolute control of Northern Pacific. In doing so, they would command its half interest in Burlington; then they would be masters of the entire West up from the Mexican border.

So Harriman and Schiff secretly began to execute

their plans. Cablegrams started humming between the Kuhn, Loeb banking house in Pine Street and its representatives in England and Germany. In Wall Street, its brokers received quiet instructions. Nobody suspected their plot.[12]

[12] Kennan: *E. H. Harriman*.

XXIII

A GREAT NORTHERN special was rushing and roaring through the night, the scream from its locomotive suddenly deadened as it swept into the opening of the long tunnel under the Cascade Range, faster, ever faster, from Seattle, heading toward the East. It had one car, and but a single passenger,— the builder of the railroad.

Swaying on his cushioned chair to the swift motion of the train, his broad body clothed in a suit that looked rumpled and shabby, his thick lips pursed thoughtfully, Hill's piercing eye was fastened on the newspaper in his hands. All about him were strewn copies of the New York dailies of the close of April, 1901.

Strange as it might seem in a man who boasted of never having set foot in the New York Stock Exchange, or bought or sold a share for speculation, Mr. Hill was scanning the market quotations.

Hill always protested that he had no more to do with Wall Street gambling than the man in the moon. He likened the scenes on the floor of the Exchange to the "ghost-dancing" of the natives out in his Indian country. He could never understand why Wall Street speculated. He was quite sincere about that. Speculation was something that was simply not embraced in his philosophy.

Yet just now it was the quotations on Northern Pacific that had fixed Hill's eye. He noted with anxiety the enormous amounts of transactions in its shares. A code telegram had informed him of a steady rise in the stock. No doubt about it, the old railroad builder was suspicious and alarmed.

When Hill and Morgan had accomplished the Burlington deal, they believed that they had checkmated their Union Pacific rivals. Morgan, indeed, had felt so secure, that he had sailed abroad, being in ill-health and exhausted after his exertions in organizing the Steel Trust. And Hill, also feeling quite satisfied, had gone to the Pacific coast.[1]

But now, alarmed by the reports he had received from his Eastern agents, Hill was hurrying back to Wall Street, to learn what was in the wind.

The old man began to figure rapidly on a scratch pad. Northern Pacific had outstanding eighty millions in common and seventy-five millions in preferred. Now Hill and the friends on whom he could depend, held thirty to forty per cent of the common.

[1] Pyle: *Life of James J. Hill.*

That was usually considered ample to control a corporation. They hadn't the majority stock,—it had not occurred to them that they would need it.[2]

The brain under that big domed head was functioning rapidly. Could this be Harriman's hand? If so, what was he after? Control of the Northern Pacific? Impossible! But that puzzling advance in price was to Hill like the steady fall of the barometer.

Hill was under no illusion as to the significance of such a counterstroke by his opponent. Harriman in command of Northern Pacific could cripple Great Northern, destroy its value, restrict its growth. Suppose the Union Pacific gained N. P. It would succeed also to a half interest in the Burlington. All the system of relations, and the scheme of traffic worked out by Hill would be suspended or destroyed.

Hot worry filled the old man's mind.[3]

So swift was Hill's journey, that he arrived in Wall Street on the third of May. He was at once closeted with his friends, Bacon and Perkins, in the offices of Drexel, Morgan & Company. Hill was thunderstruck to learn that Morgan's firm, only the day before, tempted by the high price of N. P., had unsuspectingly sold more than a million dollars' worth of its holdings. It had thus weakened the posi-

2 Pyle: *Life of James J. Hill.*   3 *Ibid.*

196

tion in Northern Pacific of those associates on whom Hill depended for support.

Hill left the offices of his bankers. He wished to make doubly sure that his suspicions were well-founded. His forehead furrowed with care, he trotted to the offices of Kuhn, Loeb & Company, to confront his onetime friend, old Jacob Schiff.

Just as some months before, Schiff had visited Hill's offices in the company of Harriman, to question him about his Burlington purchases. Now their positions were reversed. Hill was come to question Schiff concerning his intentions with respect to Northern Pacific.

Schiff, that placid gentleman, now softly stroked his beard and nodded wisely. Yes, it was true, Mr. Hill. His firm was buying N. P. on orders from the Union Pacific interests. There was a faint gleam of contemptuous triumph in the banker's eyes,—just the slightest touch of derision in his tone.

In Schiff's estimation, Morgan was a financier to be respected, if not feared; but Morgan was far away. Hill was a traffic man and railroad builder, but he was mentally an infant when confronted with the problems of Wall Street speculation.

Hill's leonine body stiffened. A somber look flashed from his eloquent eye. "But you can't get the road. My friends and myself command working control of the property!"

"That may be so," assented the banker; "but we have quite a lot of the stock ourselves now. You see [a touch of malice crept into his voice] you secretly bought up Burlington. You refused us a fair share of interest in the road. Now we're going to have our share after all. We've got a majority voice in the affairs of Northern Pacific."

But now the ever-diplomatic underwriter assumed his patriarchal air. Surely Mr. Hill would listen to the sincere advice of an old friend. Mr. Hill must realize that so great a property as the Union Pacific could not take second place in any arrangement. We are all getting to be aged men, and why should we not live out our remaining years in peace? Coöperate with us, my dear friend; your position and power will be greater than it ever was. You shall possess the kingly crown in the railroad world.[4]

Schiff ended with his favorite wisecrack—it was said to represent the philosophy of his life: "On the mountain top, all paths unite." [5]

From his immense reserve of vitality, Hill fixed the speaker with a deadly glance. He was always ready, he said, to do the fair thing by his neighbor,

[4] Pyle: *Life of J. J. Hill.*
[5] See Introduction to *Jacob H. Schiff, His Life and Letters.*

198

the Union Pacific, but he could not be bribed to wrong the men who had helped him build up the Great Northern.

So ended the conference.

Hill moodily retraced his steps to the banking house at the corner of Broad and Wall Streets. He faced the supreme hour of his life. It was late in the day. Much ground had been lost. The enemy had already gained the advantage.

Quick, a message to Morgan! But where was Morgan to be found? Morgan was caught by cable at Aix-les-Bains. For the first time he was made acquainted with the fact that control of the Northern Pacific was in danger, if not already lost.

On May 5, the laconic and historic cablegram came in answer: *"Buy 150,000 shares of Northern Pacific!"* [6]

Bacon quickly notified Hill and Perkins of the arrival of the cablegram. The men realized what those words signified. They outlined an undertaking, great, and apparently impossible of execution. They were a command to go into the open market and buy an amount of shares to convert the Hill-Morgan holdings into a majority. And the stock market was already displaying danger signals.

The purchase of 150,000 N. P. at this moment

[6] Pyle: *Life of J. J. Hill.*

meant an expenditure of some eighteen to twenty million dollars, in estimating the then prevailing market value. But this stock would cost infinitely more before the entire amount was actually bought. A deal of this magnitude and significance could not occur without rocking the financial world.[7]

But a skillful instrument was at hand, ready to execute the job,—James R. Keene, the most dangerous stock manipulator and heartless pool operator in the Street.

Keene was now commissioned by Drexel, Morgan & Company to buy the block of Northern Pacific, a difficult and delicate undertaking, capable of execution only by a trained and market-wise intelligence. Through the medium of his brokers, Talbot J. Taylor and Street & Norton, Keene "felt out the market." It was "hard," and he quickly learned the reason: Herzfeld & Stern, and other Kuhn, Loeb brokers were, under cover, picking up all the shares they could.

The master manipulator now intervened in the game. On Monday, May 6, the market was being scoured for N. P. certificates. Telegrams were flashing to all parts of the Union, bidding for the stock. The market jumped four points and closed at $125.50 a share.

[7] Pyle: *Life of J. J. Hill.*

Tuesday came, May 7, the opening of the battle. The market was swept clean of Northern Pacific. All pretense was thrown aside. The high intrigue, subtly hidden from the public, was half-revealed. N. P. leaped to $149.75, or $39.75 a share above the close of Saturday.

Meanwhile, what was Harriman doing?

It is necessary to revert to the closing days of April, that had first aroused Hill's suspicions, and caused his rush journey to Wall Street. Harriman, in action, was swift and unsparing. Out to rule or ruin. All during April, the Little Wizard, a semi-invalid, feverish and frail, quietly grabbed all the stock he could reach in this country, and, through the international banking house behind him, he picked up what he could in the investment centers of London, Amsterdam and Berlin.

Schiff had assured Harriman that Kuhn, Loeb & Company had bought a majority of the total N. P. stock issue and that the battle had been won. Harriman remained tortured by doubts, for a grave reason.

There was a joker in the pack of cards with which Hill and Harriman were playing: *The common stockholders of Northern Pacific had the right to pay off the preferred stock on January 1, of any year until 1927!*

Schiff had bought 37 million common and 42 million preferred. That gave him and his confederate a clear majority of the two classes of stock taken together; but they lacked 40,000 shares of having a majority of common. Harriman saw Hill having a chance to lick him by retiring the preferred and leaving him with a minority after all.

Morning of Saturday, May 4. Harriman, ill, at home, tossing feverishly in bed. Schiff had told him the day before of Hill's sudden arrival, and of his interview with the railroad builder. Harriman suffered cruel suspicions. Those missing 40,000 shares! Those fatal 40,000!

Suddenly Harriman grabbed the telephone by his bedside and called up the bankers in Pine Street. A response came from Heinsheimer, a partner of Schiff's. Harriman gave him an order to buy immediately "at the market," 40,000 shares of N. P. for his own account.

"All right," responded Heinsheimer.

All through that two-hour market day Harriman suffered pain and anxiety. A few moments after noon, he learned that N. P. had closed at $110. Dealings had been heavy. In relief, the railroad financier sank back on his pillow. No doubt his order had been filled; he had his coveted 40,000 shares.

Fresh anxieties on Monday morning. Still on his

sick bed, Harriman had received no confirmation of the purchase of his 40,000. Had there been a slip-up? Again he called up Heinsheimer. "Where is the report of my Saturday's order?"

Over the wire came Heinsheimer's voice, soft and plausible. It threw the dark, nervous invalid into a paroxysm of rage.

It appeared that Heinsheimer, on receiving Saturday's order, felt that he must first consult his senior, Schiff, before executing it. But old Jacob, orthodox in religion, was never in Wall Street on Saturdays. He was then at the synagogue. Heinsheimer got him later. Schiff thought it a waste of money to buy more stock. He said that he would be responsible for the non-execution of the order.

The news drove Harriman from his sick bed down to Pine Street. To his financial backer, the financier deplored the banker's tactical error. The chance to get the 40,000 shares had now passed, for the market was being swept bare of N. P. by Keene. The shares were jumping higher by the minute.[8]

The fell day of Tuesday, May 7, dawned and passed.

Both banking camps professed to have won the victory. The last lingering shares of N. P. had been picked up, but the bankers kept on buying.

[8] Kennan: *E. H. Harriman.*

Brokers were selling stock to them. But these were now "short sales." The sellers did not have the certificates to deliver. They kept selling because they believed N. P. was so high that it was bound to break; but so long as these bears could not deliver what they sold, the price of the stock rose higher and higher.

Hill and Morgan had bought contracts for their 150,000 shares. They had 30,000 more shares of common stock than was necessary for control of Northern Pacific.

On the other hand, Harriman owned some 6,000 shares more than majority control, if common and preferred were lumped together.

Hill vowed to pay off the preferred on the first of January. He would thus reduce his opponent to a minor place.

But Harriman boasted the authority for choosing a majority of the board of directors at the next meeting of N. P. He could thus prevent retirement of the preferred.

The situation was a deadly puzzle.

Bankers, financiers and their counsel argued these questions heatedly behind closed doors; but during their disputes and deliberations, they were suddenly compelled to pause. These gentlemen sensed the silent approach of a mysterious phenomenon. Overhead, above Wall Street, above the country, over the financial centers of the world, winging and wheeling in triumphant joy was the genius of the cycle, whose plans were ripened for the crowning-stroke of his orbit.

XXIV

NINTH OF MAY, 1901

THE old Stock Exchange in Broad Street had passed from the picture. While a greater trading house was being built, the Produce Exchange had given the courtesy of a portion of its floor to the Wall Street brokers.[1] In these new surroundings, one was now to witness the struggle of the Wall Street mob, caught in a web of fatality.

At the peak of the wildest bull market the Street had ever known, a stupendous fact had been driven home to the stockbrokers.[2]

Northern Pacific had been cornered!

The price advance in this stock was due solely to the fact that the two greatest banking houses of the Street had already bought up all the Northern Pacific available; but they had kept on buying, because brokers and brokers' customers were fighting the market by "selling short."

Speculators were under the influence of an emotional insanity. They lived in momentary expectation

---

[1] *Herald*, April 27-30, 1901.
[2] *Ibid*, May 8, 1901.

that the stock movement would collapse. Then they would win fortune on the bear side.

But the short seller, banking on a fall in the market, takes a tremendous risk. As he keeps selling, his broker must go through the performance of "borrowing" the actual share certificates from another broker, in order to make his deliveries the following day.

When, as in the present instance, the market has been swept clean of the stock in question, the lender of such certificates begins to charge a premium for loaning them.

Day by day, as the shorts sell, this premium rises higher and higher, even as the stock quotations rise higher and higher. This situation must be kept in mind; it explains the entire action of the Northern Pacific panic.

It was incomprehensible that a corner could actually be concerted in a property that had eighty millions par value in common stock outstanding. No such thing had ever happened.

Yet the corner was an actuality. It was proved by the crazy demonstrations in the loan crowd on the floor of the Exchange, where the brokers had to "borrow" the certificates, so that they might fulfill their deliveries on the succeeding day.

This loan crowd was now a mass of men milling about the Northern Pacific trading post. Convulsive fingers were signaling bids and offers in the sign language of the brokers. Men yelled opposing bids in one another's ears with futile desperation.

Street & Norton and Talbot J. Taylor & Company, brokers acting for Keene, had bought up nearly 150,-000 shares on Monday; they loaned out nearly the full amount by the close of the market.[8] They thus gave the short-sellers, who had borrowed these shares, a means for committing financial suicide, because these unfortunate men were unaware that those shares represented the buying order cabled from Aix-les-Bains on Sunday by J. Pierpont Morgan.

The foolish bears hoped to break the corner. They were unwilling to cover their sales with losses at the prevailing prices. They began to offer premiums for the loan of the stock certificates.

A young and vigorous broker approached the N. P. trading post with a brisk step. He was "Al" Stern, a broker for the Harriman bankers. "Who wants to borrow N. P.?" he asked, carelessly; "I have a block to lend."

Up went a shout. There was an infinitesimal pause. Then Stern's fellow-brokers charged upon him. The young man hurriedly loaned his last shares and broke away from his persecutors, with rumpled clothes.

[8] *Herald,* May 8, 1901.

But bidders were now offering seven per cent, eight per cent, and finally ten per cent, for the loan of Northern Pacific.

These bids meant that brokers would pay $1,000 for the privilege of borrowing 100 shares for 24 hours. Yet the floating supply of N. P. was practically exhausted.

Meanwhile the two great banking houses that were loaning their stock to the unfortunate men whom they had entrapped, were coining millions in profits by the hour.

At the opening of the market on Wednesday, May 8, the hidden manipulators of the corner squeezed Nipper to the high price of $180 a share.

Suddenly Talbot J. Taylor, Keene's son-in-law and representative on the floor, called in every share of Northern Pacific which his firm had loaned. Moore & Schley also called their loans.

By this action, these powerful brokers were condemning Wall Street to ruin, for there was little, if any, stock on hand. As on the previous day, the turmoil was resumed in the loan crowd, as the premium mounted.

"Seven per cent for 1,000 N. P.!"

"I'll give eight per cent for 500!"

"Ten per cent for 2,000 N. P.!"

The struggle grew fiercer, the bidding more desperate.

"Fifteen per cent for N. P.!"

"Sixteen per cent for 100!"

"I'll give twenty per cent to borrow 500 shares!"

Again the Kuhn, Loeb broker, "Al" Stern, appeared, and mounted the seat beside the Nipper trading post. Brokers leaped at him. They bid 32 per cent, 33 per cent, for Northern Pacific, but to the general consternation, the representative of the Pine Street banking house announced that he had no shares to lend. He would have to call in the loans he had made the day before.[4]

On this news, the premium jumped from 45 per cent upwards, until it touched 85 per cent. Traders actually bid this almost incredible figure, which meant that they were willing to pay the sum of $8,500 in order to borrow, for only a few hours, a certificate of railroad stock of the par value of $10,000.[5]

May 9 dawned in gloom and rain, as had many another evil day in Wall Street. Depressed lines of brokers and speculators passed down to the Produce Exchange. The stroke of the gavel that brought the market's opening was succeeded by a tumult about the Nipper trading post.[6]

[4] *Herald*, May 9, 1901. [6] *Ibid.*, May 10.
[5] *Ibid.*

There was not a man who any longer tried to buy Northern Pacific either for speculation or investment. The price of this stock had become an unknown quantity, altered by the momentary and desperate passions of men.

There were two classes of bids, "cash" and "regular." The "regular" bids were made by brokers who covered their short sales, and who bought back shares they had previously sold. "Cash" bids were made by brokers who needed the actual certificates for delivery to their creditors. "Cash" quotations were utterances of desperation; they were always higher than "regular" quotations.

At the Nipper trading post, a "regular" sale had just been made at 165, when a mob of brokers, running over from other posts, began to yelp for cash securities.

A half-crazed broker, clamoring for 200 shares of Nipper "cash," without being able to get it, offered $225 a share, and got it. Then the "regular" stock jumped between sales 46 points, from 159 to 205. In another moment it leaped to 230.

And now occurred the most remarkable stretch of stock dealing that had ever taken place on 'Change,— a stretch in which all sense of values and proportions faded into nothing.

Shares of the disputed railroad were to rise to

figures which meant calamity to unnumbered men;
and even to the present day, in old Wall Street commission houses, one may still see, framed behind
glass, upon the walls, the yellowed length of actual
ticker tape, exhibiting the unforgettable quotations.

The next cash sale had remained wavering at the
price of $300, when there was a sudden leap to $400
—a leap between sales of the full par value of the
stock. The next sale was executed at $650, in a
bound of $250 a share between cash sales. Another
sale came at $700. It was just after this transaction
that Northern Pacific common was flung abruptly up
to $1,000 a share for cash. This was a quotation
higher than that of Standard Oil in those days. The
common stock of the railroad had not brought one-
tenth of that price on the previous Saturday.[7]

This was the greatest, the most breath-taking moment that the Stock Exchange had experienced in its
century-long annals. In contemplating it, one must
place himself in the mental state of the man who, in
his profound despair, had bid the frightful sum to
make his deliveries.

The brokerage house of Street & Norton had re-
leased 300 shares at the $1,000 figure to this unfortu-
nate victim of the corner, which they, acting for

[7] *Herald*, May 10.

NINTH OF MAY, 1901

"Jim" Keene, who in turn represented J. P. Morgan & Company, had helped develop.[8]

Meanwhile, as the price of Northern Pacific had kept climbing, it was suddenly noted with horror by the traders that all other stocks were beginning to collapse. Enormous fluctuations of prices came in seconds, for to the men who had been trapped in the Northern Pacific corner, there was but one expedient left. They threw all other share possessions overboard at whatever prices they might bring.

Thus fortunes of the wealthiest families in the country dwindled away. Union Pacific fell in an instant to $105, with a net loss of $60 a share; Manhattan lost 40 points; Rock Island, 35½; Atchison, 32½; Steel common, 23 points; Steel preferred, 26¾.[9]

Then, as humanity can never be extinguished in the breasts of men, one beheld the very agents of the big banking houses, the brokers who had been whipped into line by financiers in the execution of the relentless corner, fall subject to an emotional breakdown upon the trading floor.

Tears in his eyes, Norton, the Keene broker, seeing himself surrounded by old friends, for whom the course of Northern Pacific spelled ruin, called upon God to testify to the grief he felt at their

[8] *Ibid.*   [9] *Ibid.*

predicament. One of the Kuhn, Loeb brokers bewailed the fact that he had been compelled to crucify his friends.

Meanwhile, in customers' rooms of brokerage offices throughout Wall Street, men, clustered about stock tickers, with wet eyes, stammered curses upon the heads of those whom they considered the deliberate authors of their misfortune.[10]

Men prominent in the financial world, terrified by conditions, hurried to the Morgan offices and appealed to Robert Bacon. Others expostulated with Kuhn, Loeb & Company. Half the stock commission houses in the Street faced ruin; they could not meet their contracts; besides, a weight of anger and hatred was swiftly piling up against those who were held responsible for the mischief.

The bankers were impressed; they consented to save Wall Street from the destruction that their corner had brought about; they might, indeed, in accordance with the cruel code of the Street, have extracted the extreme limit from their debtors, the last dollar of their bank balances and assets.[11]

But the bankers decreed that those who had sold them Northern Pacific stock which they could not deliver, should pay them the sum of $150 a share; this amount would release their debtors from their

[10] *Herald*, May 10.   [11] *Ibid.*

contracts; so the shorts were penalized in that sum; it represented an absolute profit to the bankers.[12]

The panic was over. Northern Pacific gradually resumed its normal value, but the shock of the corner had reverberated 'round the world, affecting the trading markets in Berlin, Hamburg, Paris and London, where no more miserable day could have been experienced than that of May 9. There, in the Street, after trading hours, in drenching rain, up to their ankles in mud and water, frightened and haggard men, brokers, speculators, dealers, clerks, huddled together, almost voiceless with alarm.

As defenders of their property, Hill and Morgan had won victory.

Schiff continued to assure Harriman that they possessed enough interest in Northern Pacific to command recognition.

A dangerous position was assumed by the two opposing groups, entertaining capabilities for working great mischief. The financiers might have continued to tear up Wall Street, engaging in endless litigation, but the sobering effect of the panic induced them to take a wiser course.

They formed an immense holding corporation, the Northern Securities Company,—which controlled securities of the properties whose ownership had been

[12] Stedman: *N. Y. Stock Exchange.*

the occasion of the struggle,—Northern Pacific and Burlington.

Hill, Harriman and their bankers believed that they had placed *finis* to a complicated problem.

But in Wall Street nothing ever ends.

The Northern Securities Company was merely one slender thread in the web of the financial district, where spinning never stops.

XXV

AN EXTRAORDINARY CIRCUMSTANCE

THREE years later, the Northern Securities Company was forcibly annulled.

This big combination had terrified the West with its potentialities for harm, and the Supreme Court had directed its dissolution. It was held to be a violation of the Anti-Trust Law and its power to restrain trade was considered unwarranted.[1]

Now Morgan and Schiff had both grown gray in the conservative schools of international finance. They were far-seeing bankers, to whom impulse, theretofore, had been a stranger. Hill and Harriman were no less far-sighted. Yet these four most powerful men in American finance, once friends and associates, had fallen apart in sudden distrust and terror of one another.

These men had lied to one another, overreached one another, threatened one another with ruin, and in doing so, they had risked the solvency of Wall Street, utterly indifferent to consequences. Their fight for control of a corporation had ended in a

---

[1] Pyle: *Life of J. J. Hill.*

great explosion on the floor of the Stock Exchange, ripping apart the financial world.

And in the end—nothing!

All that these great financiers had planned and plotted, at the close of the toil and tumult, had ended in defeat, in absolute nullification and negation. These experienced men had misjudged the spirit of their own time, for the highest tribunal had decreed that even their compromise was a violation of their country's laws.

One gives close attention to the statements these men have left behind them, scrutinizes their authorized biographies, and listens to the elucidations of their apologists,—to meet only with explanations that explain nothing.[2]

This is unquestionably an extraordinary circumstance. Nobody assumes the blame for having created the great disorder, and nobody is called to account for it. The four principals seem confused in contemplating their own acts, being as stunned and dazed as were the Wall Street financiers twenty-eight years later, when the avalanche of the Great Deflation of '29 roared about their ears.

It would be useless to hunt for an explanation of the panic of May, 1901, in such economic subterfuges

[2] *Life Story of J. Pierpont Morgan; Life of James J. Hill; Jacob H. Schiff, His Life and Letters; E. H. Harriman.*

as over-extension of loans, foreign liquidations, inflation of stocks, excessive credits. As we progress with our observations, it appears to become plainer and plainer that the panic is a man-made proposition.

The high gamblers of 1929, with millions of ready cash in hand, utilized the functions of the existing Wall Street machinery; they ran up stocks and copped the public's money; few of them had ever created anything substantial; they merely played a wild hazard. The Street, in our time, is no more conscientious than it ever was.

In justice to the four masters of Wall Street who, in 1901, brought on catastrophe, it must be said that they did not deliberately cause the corner in Northern Pacific. The corner came as a result of the struggle between Morgan and Hill, Schiff and Harriman. These financiers simply ignored the public, although in the end they did not hesitate to profit from its distress. But it must be admitted in their favor that these men had established permanent industries, and founded important transportation companies.

Yet, in effect, the playboys of 1929, and the railway schemers of 1901, merely repeated, in their days, the performances of a lesser group of men who, in promoting their ill-starred monopolies, ushered in the panic of '93. And a generation before these, we saw Seney, Eno and Ward, the financial adventurers who sponsored the disasters of '84. They, in turn, had been preceded by men of still lesser note and repute in '57,—Schuyler, the railway stock forger, accompanied by men not potential or even instinctive criminals, but who, transformed by circumstances into thieves and defaulters, became the instigators of an emotional catastrophe.

In reviewing events at the close of '93, we observed that, in the human scope of the panic, its leaders exhibited similar limitations of judgment, misdirected energies and even rogueries; but it was through their efforts that the wheels of the cycle were set in motion.

Generally men of experience and training, they fail to realize the inevitable outcome of their actions; they appear to be unconscious instruments, pushed on by some driving power; and the nature of this hidden power, this secret force, is something that we shall have to try to discover.

VIII

THE BATTLING BANKERS

XXVI

MEN OF 1907

AN interval of six years,—and one was to witness the greatest of all panics.[1]

This was first an idea in the mind of a highly practical business man. His offices were on the eleventh floor of a gray stone building, solid as a prison, in lower Broadway. Normally, the director of the Standard Oil Company, Henry H. Rogers, displayed a rather kindly good will; but just now his plans had been interrupted, and his eyes had assumed a terrible, almost tigerish expression.

Rogers had watched his company's balance sheet growing until its accumulated millions cried for investment; then he had gone to the booming State of Montana and placed its surplus in copper mines; subsequently he organized the Amalgamated.[2]

The National City Bank had launched the Amalgamated's $155,000,000 stock capital. J. P. Morgan & Company had financed the issue. No such eminent

[1] *Commercial and Financial Chronicle*, January, 1908.
[2] *Herald*, Feb. 4, 1906. *Chronicle*, Jan, 1901.

sponsors had ever backed a mining enterprise. So
the world went copper mad.[3]

Suddenly the boom turned sour. The Amalgamated syndicate, cornering its copper at a high, artificial price, could find no buyers for its product. The
pool crashed, and Amalgamated dropped from $130
to $60 a share.[4]

Our copper men rarely see further than their
noses. They are good panic-breeders. In 1929 they
also pooled their metal and tried to keep it at twenty-
four cents a pound. Once more the buyers went on
strike. Then the red metal dropped to less than ten
cents, and Anaconda went into a tail-spin, slumping
from $140 to $33 a share. History had blindly
repeated itself.

However, at the time when Amalgamated took its
nose-dive in 1907, the disillusioned investors turned
vindictively upon the National City Bank. They
scored this depository for having sponsored a mining
venture.

The City Bank, in those days, occupied a plain
building in Wall Street, fronted with flat, stained
marble slabs. Before a desk, perched upon a
small, raised platform, sat a man, slight, dark, with a

[3] Stedman: *N. Y. Stock Exchange.*
[4] Alexander Dana Noyes: *Forty Years of American Finance,*
1909.

rather elegant figure. He was strangely sensitive.[5]

James Stillman had an almost feline patience in the pursuit of his purpose. Had he an enemy, he would wait immobile for years, if need be, to strike him down. He was proud, also, and unused to censure. Public criticism hurt him like a scorpion's sting.[6]

So there they were in their Wall Street strongholds,—Stillman, immobile, Rogers, ferocious in his rage, both nursing their grudge against an individual whom they held accountable for the indignities that were being heaped upon them for their ill-starred flotation of Amalgamated.

The man who had won their resentment was a miner out in distant Montana. One might have viewed him there on a raw November night, standing on the steps of the Court House in Butte,[7] speaking earnestly to a big assembly of mining men. He was a good orator. The flare of acetylene lights threw into prominence his bold, dashing figure, his long, handsome face, distinguished by a challenging and provocative smile.

Wall Street, he said, called him a mining pirate, whose sole assets were a hundred lawsuits. But the

[5] Anna Robeson Burr: *The Portrait of a Banker*, 1927.
[6] *Ibid.*
[7] F. Augustus Heinze: *The Political Situation in Montana*, 1900-1902.

men before him knew better. They knew the terrible persecution he was suffering at the hands of the Amalgamated. He had invested half a million in the Nipper. But injunctions had shut him out from mining and giving employment to his men. He had found a copper mine in the Minnie Healy, but Wall Street had jockeyed him out of it. He had bought half of the Snohomish,—he had made a mine there, but they had snatched it from his hands.[8]

"If they crush me to-day," cried the orator, with his reckless air, "they'll crush you to-morrow. They'll cut your wages, and raise the tariff in the company store. No man or woman ever heard that F. Augustus Heinze played a friend or partner false. My fight is yours. We sink or swim together!"[9]

The appeal was irresistible. The miners had listened spellbound. Then a great murmur from rough throats ended in yipping yells of applause.

Such sentiments traveled promptly back to Wall Street.

What hurt most was that Heinze was telling the truth. When the Amalgamated people tied him up in litigation, he swore to fight them with their own weapons. He and his brother, Arthur, bought up

[8] F. Augustus Heinze: *The Political Situation in Montana*, 1900-1902.
[9] *Ibid.*

226

disputed titles and began countersuits. Strikes, riot-
ing and violence ensued at the mines, until the copper industry was in a snarl.

Rogers tried to compromise with Heinze by offering him $250,000 for his claims. The miner laughed
in the financier's face. The copper war continued for
seven long years, but at the end of it, Standard Oil
capitulated. It bought the Heinze properties at a
price variously given as from fifteen to twenty-five
millions.[10]

In the mining world, such figures must be swallowed with a grain of salt; but, at any rate, Heinze
had beaten the strongest banking coterie in the world,
—the Standard Oil-City Bank-Morgan group.
He had compelled them to the humiliation of surrender. But no sooner were his hard-won millions
in his hands, than his thoughts turned to Wall Street.
He was a banker in Montana, and his bold spirit
leaped at the thought of invading and disputing the
financial world of his recent foes.

In New York, Heinze fell in with a genius of contrivers. Charles W. Morse at that time possessed
everything that froze upon the Hudson River, and
nearly everything that floated upon the Atlantic seaboard. Morse owned the Hudson Navigation Company, the Metropolitan Line, the Eastern Steamship

[10] *Herald*, Feb. 14, 1906.

Company, the Ward Line and the Clyde Line,—in all, a fleet of seventy-four ships.

But in his manipulations of American Ice and the Consolidated Steamship Company, Morse needed banks. He already owned the Garfield National. Now he bought more banks. In January, 1901, he bought the Produce Exchange Bank and the Bank of New Amsterdam. By April, he obtained the Twelfth Ward Bank; seven days later, the Bank of the State of New York; in October, the National Broadway. Seventeen days after, he was owner of the National Commercial; in December he possessed the National Bank of North America. Two days later, Morse won his ninth New York bank, the Fourteenth Street; within ten months he owned interests in the Trust Company of America and the Van Norden Trust Company.

Now all this has a very familiar ring. Mergers of steamship companies, making for lower operating costs. Consolidations of banks, branch banking, advantages of chains of banks. Why, the financial philosophers taught us in 1929 that these were the inventions, the discoveries, of the New Era.

But in these earlier years, Wall Street professed to be horrified by Morse's manipulations. He was using the stock and surplus of one bank in order to buy the next one.[11]   He was hypothecating and re-hypothecating his securities in depositories in New England.   All this seemed very criminal.

And Morse was now being associated with ambitious partners.   With his coöperation, Heinze, the daring adventurer, had made himself president of the Mercantile National and he was interested in the Consolidated Bank and a chain of other institutions.

These two banker-adventurers were joined by Edward Russell Thomas, a young sportsman.   The father of Thomas had left him an income of $180,-000 a year.   This adventurous young man had concerted a two-million-dollar corner in cotton.   He was owner of champion thoroughbreds; and now he had become a power in the Hamilton Bank, the Consolidated National, the Mechanics' & Traders'.

Then Charles T. Barney attached himself to this group.   He was president of the Knickerbocker Trust Company, with its resources of more than seventy millions.   He had built its main office, at Fifth Avenue and Thirty-fourth Street, in the form of a marble temple.   With its eleven Corinthian columns, it was conspicuous for its architectural beauty.

Morse was the cleverest and most resourceful of all these men, whose invasion had come to plague the

[11] Alexander Dana Noyes: *Forty Years of American Finance*, 1909.

229

Street. He was utilizing the banks controlled by Heinze, Thomas and Barney, in making loans on behalf of his corporations, American Ice and Consolidated Steamship. He commanded a dozen banks and trust companies in New York, three in Maine, and two in New Hampshire.

The great Wall Street bankers, entrenched behind their granite walls, supported by their feudal traditions, watched all these proceedings with misgivings. They were confronted by newcomers who were about to contend the ownership of their long-established monarchy.

Indeed, the Street had become a potential battleground. Two powerful forces faced each other, in the fashion of ancient armies about to dispute the passage of a river.

In the one camp, the big underwriting banks and the old-line trust companies: the National City Bank, the National Bank of Commerce, the First National, the Hanover National, the Farmers' Loan & Trust, the United States Trust, the New York Trust and the Guaranty Trust, which was the institution of the Standard Oil. These institutions were dominated by J. Pierpont Morgan and his partner, Robert Bacon; by William Rockefeller, the genial speculator; by Rogers, the man with tiger's blood, and Stillman, the subtle, whose enmity never slumbered.

And facing them, one saw the indomitable in-
vaders, in their financial fortresses: the National
Bank of North America, the Mercantile Trust, the
Knickerbocker Trust,—Morse, the genius of manipulators, Heinze, who had once brought the strength
of Wall Street to its knees.

These years were very prosperous. The Western
railroads sold big share issues. The paper securities
of the Great Northern, the Northern Pacific, the St.
Paul, were swept up to high levels. Heinze exploited his new corporation, United Copper, with its
fifty millions of capital. He bet $25,000 with one of
his friends, that United would soon sell higher in
the market than its rival, Amalgamated.

The star of Charles T. Barney, especially, seemed
to be in the ascendant. With a personal fortune of
nine millions, he indulged his tastes for luxury; his
entertainments in his Park Avenue residence, deco-
rated by the talented hand of Stanford White, were
the social events of the time.

In 1906 came the San Francisco disaster, with a
property loss of $350,000,000.

The year 1907 opened with strained and mysterious movements in the money market. The Street
was constantly disturbed by President Roosevelt's
animus against unscrupulous men of large wealth.[12]

[12] *Chronicle,* Jan.-March, 1907.

XXVII

F. AUGUSTUS HEINZE won his exultant wager, the $25,000 stake, on October 14. His stock pool shot United Copper to $60 a share. Amalgamated was then selling at $54. The expert miner's victory was the cradle of grave events.

The pool in United was managed by the firm of Gross & Kleeberg, and the heavy buying was being executed through the Stock Exchange house of Otto Heinze & Company. The Heinze-Morse-Thomas chains of banks were making heavy loans on United collateral.

But hidden bears now began to raid United. The Heinze brothers laid a snare for them; they concerted a corner in the stock; then they sprang their trap; unexpectedly they demanded the delivery of United stock certificates; their plan was to uncover the identity of the bear raiders.

Admirable in theory, this scheme failed in execution. Heinze had neglected to provide proper banking facilities for paying for the incoming shares.

An avalanche of United certificates was flung into

the offices of Gross & Kleeberg and Heinze and Company. The pool managers were disconcerted. Unable to obtain cash, both firms announced their suspension. United shares broke from sixty dollars to ten dollars, and the preferred from seventy-four to twenty. Morse's Consolidated Steamship bonds sank in the market. The Street was demoralized. It heard that the banker-adventurers were embarrassed.[1]

Secret instructions went out to all banks. Loans must be called on securities of all companies with which Heinze, Morse and Thomas were associated. Stocks crashed.

Who had broken the copper corner? Who had won back the millions that Heinze had once cozened out of Wall Street? Don't let us all guess at once.

The moment had come for which a dark, silent man had been waiting, on the raised platform in the City Bank.

A committee of the Clearing House Association gathered. Its members included representatives of the Standard Oil-City Bank-Morgan group. Heinze was called before them. These gentlemen gave him the curt command to resign from the Mercantile Bank. He was told that he must place the resignations of his directors in the hands of the committee; he must sell out his stock interests in every

[1] *Herald*, Oct. 17, 1907.

233

bank in New York. Refusal to obey meant that the Clearing House would withdraw its protection from the Mercantile and the Consolidated; in fact, Heinze's chain of banks would fall to ruin.

The Montana miner bitterly protested. He charged that insinuations that his bank's surplus was impaired, had been spread to start a run upon the institution. He asked that, at least, he be permitted to draw $300,000 from his own bank to send it to the aid of his State Savings Bank, in Butte. His inquisitors laughed at his presumption. The bank in the Far West, with four millions in deposits, closed its doors that day. Heinze and his directors had to submit to orders.[2]

The following day was Saturday, October 19. The eyes of Wall Street were focused upon three Morse corporations, the National Bank of North America, the New Amsterdam and the Fourteenth Street banks. Lines of disquieted depositors gathered before their doors.

The Clearing House committee called Morse before them. The great manipulator made a terrific fight to retain his hold on his depositories. Eyes flashing, he exclaimed: "Gentlemen, I am worth eleven millions. I defy you to destroy the strength of that capital!"[3]

[2] *Herald*, Oct. 19.   [3] *Ibid.*, Oct. 21.

Empty boast! The talented contriver was dragooned into quitting every bank and trust company with which his name had been linked.

Sunday came. Old Trinity was tolling as churchgoers went to worship; but fifteen bankers were seated in the Clearing House in Cedar Street. Heinze and Morse had been accounted for; their depositories had been taken over by the rulers of the Street. Now Edward B. Thomas, the youthful banker-sportsman, received his sentence. He was harshly commanded to sell out his interests in the Hamilton and the Consolidated.

The Street was becoming uneasy. The operations of the banker-invaders had been indiscreet, no doubt; but was the rancor with which the established interests pursued them less ill-advised?

The storm seemed clearing on the succeeding day. Stocks were recovering, when suddenly there descended a more fearful blow.

On this Monday, J. Pierpont Morgan returned to the city from a visit to the South. It might have been a mere coincidence that, a few hours later, the National Bank of Commerce, of which this banker was the dominant director, gave notice that it would no longer act as clearing agent for the Knickerbocker Trust, of which Charles T. Barney was president.[4]

[4] *Ibid.,* Oct. 22.

235

"Harry" B. Hollins, an intimate companion of Morgan's, now called a special meeting of the Knickerbocker directorate. He launched into a bitter personal attack upon the president. Barney, he said, was overextended in his personal obligations and if the banker's loans were called, he might be unable to meet them. Finally Hollins charged Barney with his most deadly offense: his friendship with Charles W. Morse.

At the conference table, Barney sat silent, with eyes somber and apprehensive. As he rose to speak in his defense, he reminded his directors that when he had taken hold of the Knickerbocker, its resources were only fourteen millions, but under his management, they had gone up to seventy. His loans to Morse were negligible, and not in excess of $200,000. He had not advanced more than a million on American Ice collateral.

Barney was heard in silence. There was no attempt to dispute the banker's assertions, nor was there any argument about them. Hollins uttered a peremptory command: Barney must immediately resign and take up all his loans; otherwise the Clearing House banks would not advance a dollar to aid his company.[5]

Barney was sensitive, but also sensible. He bowed

[5] Carl Hovey: *Life Story of J. Pierpont Morgan.*

to the inevitable. He told his directors that if they felt that some one else could serve their interests better, he would accept the terms imposed upon him.

But now the directors themselves fell prey to consternation. They decided to hold an evening conference at Sherry's, in Fifth Avenue. The fashionable restaurant, on this autumn evening, was filled with diners; but laughter and talking ceased as time passed. The men from Wall Street were arriving. Anxious gossip spread slowly concerning the conference that was being held behind closed doors in the assembly room.[6]

In the meeting room were directors of the Knickerbocker, presidents of the allied trust companies, and two partners of the Morgan banking house,— Charles W. Steele and George W. Perkins. The Knickerbocker would have to clear for itself on the morrow, and in its vaults that night were eight millions in cash. Was this enough with which to face the coming day?

Men got to their feet and argued this question. Some advised closing the doors of the company. Many were unwilling to see this done.

Hours passed. The session became stormy. Doors of the room were no longer guarded. Persons

[6] *Ibid.*

slipped in from the supper room and shouted un-
heeded advice.

But slowly a measure developed for the rescue of
the depository. The allied trust companies pledged
themselves to provide ten millions in cash. An appeal was made to the Morgan partners. An impression prevailed, or the statement was actually made,
that a group of bankers, in which Morgan's name
was mentioned, stood ready to advance five millions
more.[7]

Then the gathering dispersed into the now deserted Avenue. Despite assurances that fifteen millions would be provided on the morrow, uneasy fore-
bodings weighted all minds, here, in the emptiness of
midnight, in the windiness and chill of October. The
day that had passed had left its blot of vengeance.
It was to bear its folly's fruit.[8]

Tuesday morning, when the doors of the Knickerbocker branch in lower Broadway were opened, bank
messengers streamed inside. They were followed by
agents of high financiers and market operators. Slips
of paper were shoved through the wickets of paying
tellers. Few words were spoken. One heard only
the sliding of bank notes, the tinkling of glass jars
containing sponges, with which the clerks moistened
their fingers as they counted.

[7] *Herald*, Oct. 22.   [8] Burr: *Portrait of a Banker.*

One check for $1,500,000 was paid over the counter. It was collected by the Hanover National, of which James Stillman and William Rockefeller were directors; another check for a million came from the Trust Company of America, and then a messenger from the New Amsterdam National presented a draft for $600,000.[9]

These were strange proceedings for Wall Street banks which had balances with the Knickerbocker. Were these depositories not pledged, or at least in duty bound, to support this institution? How could it be supposed to survive such heavy withdrawals?

Up in Fifth Avenue, steps below the pillared entrance were filled with depositors. The counting-room was crowded. The line at the wickets of paying tellers wound along the sides of the office and out toward the doors. The run was on in deadly earnest. Bank bills had been piled ready to hand in the vaults. Mounds of green and yellow bills melted from tops of long desks behind glass barricades, framed in brass and steel.

The bank's directors were in their board room, considering ways of getting more ready cash; their motor cars were scouring the city for money, which they were trying to accumulate by selling securities.

A. Foster Higgins, the new president, who had

[9] *Herald,* Oct. 23.

taken Barney's place, visited J. Pierpont Morgan in the latter's banking house. The old gentleman pleaded hard with Morgan. He recalled the memory of that July day in '84, when they had joined in founding the Knickerbocker Trust. Higgins, himself, had been one of the new directors then, and Morgan one of the largest shareholders. The aged banker argued that, in the final sense, the Knickerbocker was their own company, since they had sponsored its creation. But the Knickerbocker had not yet been succored and the financier reminded the great banker of the many times Morgan had gone to the rescue of other depositories in distress.

Morgan sat in his chair, in his characteristic attitude, hat on the back of his head, smoking the black cigar fashioned from tobacco grown on his Cuban plantation. He shook his head: "I can't be called on all the time. I've got to stop somewhere." [10]

Old man Higgins turned and left.

Meanwhile, how were the runs progressing at the trust company's offices?

Ah, treachery! Betrayal! The Knickerbocker's eight millions had melted like snow. And those promised fifteen millions, where were they? All pledges made the previous night at Sherry's had been defaulted; all covenants had been broken. The

[10] Hovey: *Life of J. Pierpont Morgan.*

allied trust companies had not tendered one dollar
of the ten millions to which they had bound themselves. Quite the contrary. Their messengers had
been amongst the first to present their heavy drafts
to the paying tellers.[11] The five millions guaranteed
by the banking group had faded into the figment of
elusive words.

No bank in the city would cash the Knickerbocker's
checks. A shudder passed through Wall Street.
Barney's company had fallen victim to a spasm of
apprehension sweeping over the city.

Shortly after noon, at the Knickerbocker's lower
Broadway office, a messenger from a Wall Street
bank tried to cash a draft for one million. The paying teller hesitated. Then he returned the check.
There was not sufficient cash left to pay it. He
pulled down the green window shade behind his
wicket. This was a sign that all payments had ended,
and the waiting messengers ran swiftly away to carry
news of the suspension to their home offices.

At the same hour, at the fashionable headquarters
in Fifth Avenue, the last pile of bills had been
brought up from the vaults. A bank officer mounted
a chair to announce that no more checks would
be honored. Wickets of the tellers snapped shut.
Waiting lines disintegrated.

[11] *Herald*, Oct. 23.

Now the Harlem and Bronx branches, cleaned out of ready specie, called madly for funds on the main office. Then came news of the suspension to Harlem. The depositors' rooms were immediately cleared and closed. When the mob in the Bronx learned that their bank was broken, there came sudden, shrill cries of despair, deep curses and maledictions in Italian.

Wall Street had siphoned the Knickerbocker's millions from its vaults before the small fry uptown had gained a fair chance at its few thousands or miserable hundreds.

The Street experienced its deepest sensation when the Knickerbocker closed its doors, for that happening was the greatest single catastrophe that had yet occurred in the United States. Sixty millions of deposits, owed to individuals, companies and corporations, were in arrear, withdrawn from circulation, tied up for some distant, undated period.

The Knickerbocker's shares, which until recently had commanded a price of $1,300, were being hawked on the Curb for $500, with no takers.

There was a convulsive movement on 'Change, with a violent advance in call money to seventy per cent; but funds were scant.

It was already realized that the false faith shown to the unfortunate trust company, the abandonment of a solvent depository to its fate, had been a mistake

242

in judgment. Heavy penalties were to be the cost of an act of blind exasperation and resentment.

Panic fear was already written upon the faces of hurrying throngs.

In London, American stocks fell on wild reports by cable.

XXVIII

A GAME OF "LOUIS"

ON that night, in a small cabinet hung with renaissance tapestries, a lonely old man sat shuffling cards in a pack. He was laying them out on the table before him,—first the four kings and then the four aces, in horizontal rows.

On the wall, close beside this man, were ancient Dutch and Flemish drawings, while on high loomed great paintings from the brushes of men dead since ages, in deep, rich colors sombered by time.

A little whiter the hair at the temples, the eyes more lack-luster; a trifle more flushed the bulbous nose, but still the commanding presence, the figure large and retaining its masterful air.

Morgan at seventy. A far cry back to that day, fifty years long syne, when he, in the panic of '57, a tall young fellow, not overbright, had arrived in New York to represent his father's London banking house. Now he was the great man of Wall Street. His word was law.

Morgan's command of capital was very wide. Funds of the eight largest banks were at his disposal and seven trust companies were under his direct control. His banking power aggregated more than a billion. Total resources, in which his influence was paramount, in railroads and industries, were reckoned at ten billions.[1]

The player at patience, absorbed in his game of "Louis," was now laying out his foundation cards,—the twelve auxiliaries. Puzzled, calculating by turns, he kept his colorless eyes riveted on each bit of illuminated cardboard as he drew it from the pack, estimating its potential value as he placed it down, remaining deeply absorbed, contemplative, oblivious to all else in the great world that hummed about him.

It was very late,—midnight must have been near or it was close to passing. From the room adjoining came murmuring voices, punctuated now and again by subdued exclamations.

Such, on this early morning hour of October 23d, was the scene in the art gallery, known as the "library," that Morgan had built to shelter his collections, his Babylonian records, Gallo-Roman and Merovingian antiquities, paintings, porcelains and illuminated manuscripts.

Some hours earlier, carriages had rounded the corner of Madison Avenue and swung into Thirty-sixth Street. Visitors, crossing the stone walk that cut

[1] Carl Hovey: *Life Story of J. Pierpont Morgan.*

through the oblong of green lawn, had cast suspicious glances toward a shadowed group huddled
beside the bronze entrance doors. They had felt
relieved only when they were safely in the hall,
flanked by green marble columns, vaulted by the sky-
light, through whose glass the stars of the firma-
ment shone as if seen in the empty air.[2]

Frick had come, with his promise of big sums,
and Harriman, piercing eyes behind bright glasses
on his narrow face, offering his aid. Lastly dark
Stillman, dressed with his usual studied care, telling
of ten millions of Standard Oil money to be loaned
through the City Bank.

Stationed on the hearthrug, Morgan had listened
to his friends. Apparently they spoke without concern, but looking closely, one could detect the trem-
bling of an eye, the slight twitching of a hand. Wall
Street would be tossed about as if by an earthquake
to-morrow. What was to be done? Should they
support the weaker companies, or let the giddy panic
run its course?

Ostensibly, Morgan was open to argument.
"What do you think?" he demanded of one visitor.
The answer was a fear that the Street might not
survive the currency drain. Shrugging this objection
aside, the banker turned to his partners, but they

[2] See Hovey: *Life Story of J. Pierpont Morgan.*

were too diplomatic to assert an opinion in his presence.

Then the master of the library expelled the smoke from his fragrant Santa Clara tobacco. He quietly expressed his views. The fact that the Knickerbocker had closed its doors, to his mind, was an event of small importance, rich and great as the depository had been. He was quite willing to let the newer trust companies go under.[3] They had no business in the financial picture.

Then Morgan paused to ask the judgment of another of his friends.

This man expressed his belief that matters were going to be difficult. The number of failures would mount daily, and what might not happen if they let a great many depositories go down? There was another aspect to the question: the public appetite had been whetted by railroad revelations and insurance scandals. Wall Street's attitude of non-assistance might prove difficult of explanation on the witness stand to inquisitive Senators.[4]

Morgan thoughtfully fingered his cigar. He knew there were men here with agile mentalities, and brighter minds than his. But he had courage and character. He was the man for final decisions.

[3] Ibid.
[4] Burr: Portrait of a Banker.

Finally he exclaimed with an air of imperious dis-
taste: "Why should I go into all that? My affairs
are in order. I've done enough. I won't take on
anything more,—unless—"

The hand which held the roll of Santa Clara tobacco gave a flourish. The others perfectly understood the gesture. That "unless" meant: "Unless I
get what I want out of it!" [5]

Morgan now turned his back on his guests. It
was not his custom to linger during discussions of
plans which preceded actual decisions. He secluded
himself in his cabinet. There he bent his powerful
mind upon the game of "Louis." It was a solace.
It had no irritations. When the pack is played, you
pick up the auxiliaries, without shuffling, and deal
them out again.[6]

The Street was rocking on its foundation stones.
The financial world might be tumbling about the
ears of some of the weak commanders. What did
that matter? Morgan selected his cards anew from
the pack.

The banker remained so engrossed that he was
quite unaware of having an observer. Only one
man would have ventured to intrude upon him.
Stillman had come in silently, and a fugitive and

---

[5] Burr: *Portrait of a Banker.*   [6] *Ibid.*

cynical smile flitted over his lips as he watched the player at solitaire.

There is a tradition that Morgan saved the Street in 1907. For two decades the point was never doubted or disputed; but after Morgan and Stillman had passed away, it was learned that the latter reserved this credit to himself. This posthumous contention became known in the publication of Stillman's biography.[7] Then it was disclosed that the proud, sensitive banker had bitterly resented hearing himself referred to as Morgan's "lieutenant" in the crisis. Stillman knew that to differ with Morgan and carry one's point was a triumph that had been achieved by few; but he felt that he had overcome this seeming impossibility. Yet this fact should remain unknown until after his death. *It was through Stillman that Wall Street had been saved!*

So the City Bank's president began to speak, as he watched the player at "Louis." His words bore upon that last unspoken phrase of Morgan's: "I'll undertake nothing, unless I get what I want."

Stillman knew what Morgan wanted, and he elaborated a means by which the dangers of the situation could be averted. The banker appealed to the other's pride and his love of power. He mentioned the name of an erratic financier who had once

[7] *Ibid.*

humiliated the master of Wall Street. This financier could be banished from the Street. Stillman named a corporation whose possession Morgan desired; he named a trust company which, if placed in peril, could give Morgan what he craved. The two of them could dragoon the Street into saving the depository which they would place in jeopardy.

Morgan listened to these counsels, poising his cards in his hand, calculating their values, with a grunt of approval, a nod of dissent, at intervals. Now at Louis, if at the third deal you have failed in placing all the cards on their respective foundations, you have lost the game.

Was it for this reason, or was it because Stillman had convinced him, that the player, raising his eyes to his companion with a look of understanding, suddenly, impatiently, threw the entire pack upon the table?

Followed by Stillman, Morgan strolled back into the meeting room. The time had come to lay results before him. Stillman spoke first. From his supple mind came words strong, clear and persuasive, guided by adroit reasoning.[8]

When fire threatens a city, then, under the guidance of a directing mind, firemen dynamite some large, yet unharmed building, to save their mimic

[8] Burr: *Portrait of a Banker.*

world; so now the bankers in Morgan's library were to direct the movement of the storm that was to break upon the Street in hours to succeed the coming dawn.

Faces blanched. Eyes lidded over their hidden confusion and uneasiness. One of the bankers left the library to give the news to the group of journalists huddled beside the entrance doors. This spokesman whispered in the darkness. He placed into the hands of the newspaper men the dynamite that was to be exploded in Wall Street. Bearing it with them, they flitted into the night.

But above and beyond this scheme of destruction, hidden from public knowledge, there remained concealed something even more deeply calculated, more profound.

XXIX

A GREAT OBJECT LESSON

WHEN the first blow of the Great Deflation fell upon Wall Street in October, 1929, we saw the brokers bewildered, the financiers flabbergasted, the speculators stupefied.

But twenty-two years earlier, on this October morning in 1907, these people had the scare of their lives.

The news presses had thundered out an official statement, issued by the bankers gathered in the Morgan library a few hours before: *They were examining the affairs of the Trust Company of America. They had organized a syndicate, which would provide money to protect it, should a run come to that depository!* [1]

Now the Trust Company of America was not imminently in danger; it had resources of $77,000,-000; its surplus was ten millions; but the depository was being sacrificed for the common good.

Was there another reason for the deliberate

[1] *Herald,* Oct. 24, 1907. *Chronicle,* Jan., 1908, in retrospect of 1907.

252

A Great Object Lesson

singling out of this institution? In its vaults it held, as collateral for a frozen loan, the securities of a great and rich enterprise. Powerful interests desired this corporation, and they were not unwilling to devise means of getting it into their possession.

The mention of this trust company's name, in a public statement, on this particular morning, the thinly-veiled invitation to start a run upon it, had the intended effect of a detonation.

Men can face the expected with stoicism; but they are terrified by the unknown.

Before business hours, thirty city policemen posted themselves in front of the Trust Company of America's building on the south side of Wall Street, between Broad and William. Twenty mounted officers began to patrol the street.

Then the mob came down.

In the fall days of 1929, the motion-picture men picked up some lively scenes in the financial district, but they had nothing on the still-camera men of 1907.

From Broadway, streaming far along Wall Street, through Nassau, Broad and William Streets, people swarmed, packed elbow to elbow, massed from houseline to houseline. Over their heads clanged the gong of terror.

Blackening the steps of the Sub-Treasury, these

253

folk filled windows of office buildings, and even their rooftops. In the street, visible only above heads and shoulders, mounted men kept the multitude in motion.

The public had been assured that the Knickerbocker would be saved; but the Knickerbocker, betrayed, had gone under in two hours. The pledge made that the Trust Company of America would be protected was now lightly tossed aside; there was a conviction that its seventy-seven millions would also be withheld from their true owners.

The long "runs" had begun that were to terrify that generation.

The queue, forming before the doors of the trust company, stretched eastward to William Street, turned the corner, extended down to Exchange Place and then halfway up that block to Broad Street.

A similar queue besieged the company's Colonial branch in Broadway.

Desperate runs followed upon the Lincoln Trust and the Fifth Avenue Trust, uptown.

To these succeeded the deadly "silent runs," in the form of heavy withdrawals, from nearly all the depositories in the city.

All this was according to plan. Morgan personally made all the bankers contribute to a common fund, under the penalty that if they did not do so, assistance would be lacking when the pinch came home to them.

Every afternoon George W. Perkins issued his autocratic commands. Each bank in the Street was thus compelled to advance a cash sum daily to help out the Trust Company of America. That distressed depository was not to be abandoned, however; it was simply to be gutted.[2]

For weeks these runs continued unabated.

Wall Street seemed to rock. Galvanic currents swept the Street.

Men staggered from the doors of the Stock Exchange, the fright of ruin frozen in their unseeing eyes. Men, known for their foresight and keen wits, committed amazing acts. A bank officer abandoned in a counting-room a satchel stuffed with a half million in securities; he wandered back again; the certificates were restored to him; he merely mumbled that nobody would have stolen them, because four per cent bonds were unsalable.

George B. Cortelyou, Roosevelt's Secretary of the Treasury, witnessed these scenes from behind a window in the Sub-Treasury. He rushed orders to Washington; but the announcement that the Treasury Department was lodging twenty-five millions in

[2] Carl Hovey: *Life Story of J. Pierpont Morgan.*

local banks, made no impression upon the lengthening queues.[3]

Nobody believed any longer in promises or pledges.

The Hamilton and Twelfth Ward banks suspended.

Receivers were appointed for the Knickerbocker; all hope seemed lost there.

Five Brooklyn depositories gave up the struggle; their liabilities aggregated twenty-one millions.

Sixteen savings banks in Manhattan took advantage of the sixty days' rule to save their resources.

The great Union Trust of Providence suspended.

One day, on the Stock Exchange, call money seemed to vanish. Bids of 100 per cent brought none to sight. Twenty millions were needed by two o'clock.

Fearful sights, then, in the secrecy of banking parlors. Dignified and stately men, whitehaired heads of old commission houses, pleaded, implored, wept and kneeled on the floor before their bankers, begging for aid, unless they were to be ruined that day, unless they were to beggar their customers.

Stillman, Morgan and Baker were told of the dilemma of the brokers. These bankers could not

[3] *Herald*, Oct. 24.

permit the closing of the Exchange, for that would
have placed a stop to their own business. Telephone
bells tinkled throughout the district. A money pool
of twenty-five millions was instantly pledged.[4] The
loan crowd on the Exchange floor was swept with
lunacy on the arrival of this money.

This was some panic.

The speechless, silent runs lasted all through November. On late, graying afternoons of dying Saturdays, when dark, threatening cloud formations
massed in anger over Wall Street, and chill winds
shuddered up Broad Street from the Bay, and twi-
lights had come early, one saw, stretching through
the Street, the historical and classic queue. Boys, old
men and shawl-wrapped women, resting on ledges of
the curb, seated on stools, straddling improvised
benches and waiting in dull-faced patience.

Waiting before the doors of the Trust Company of
America, through dreary autumn nights, until the
Sabbath dawned; remaining on post through Sunday
night till Monday came, with its banking hour. For
then they would be at the head of the line at the
paying tellers' wickets.

During these runs, the Trust Company of America had paid out 34 millions, and the Lincoln Trust
12 millions; then ultimatums were delivered to both

[4] *Chronicle*, Jan., 1908, in retrospect of 1907.

institutions. They were told that they must surrender all their unpledged assets to the ruling
bankers. On those conditions only, would funds be
provided for the remaining depositors. Cruel terms,
but they were accepted.

Now, stage by stage, the plan had been developed,
born in the counsels made by Stillman to the player
of "Louis" in Morgan's cabinet, that night following the downfall of the Knickerbocker Trust. Stillman had named a trust company which, placed in
peril, must grant Morgan what he wished: that had
been the Trust Company of America. Stillman had
named a corporation which Morgan desired: that
was the Tennessee Coal & Iron Company. The
banker had mentioned a bold, but erratic financier,
whom Morgan wished to banish from the Street: that
financier was John W. Gates.

When Gates, the "Steel Wire King," first arrived
from the West, fashionable young bucks decreed him
guilty of the sin of wearing distasteful attire, blue
shirts, with white standing collars, large-checked
suits, topped off with shiny silk hats. They rejected
him from the New York Yacht Club, blackballed him
from the Union League. Gates revenged himself by
crucifying his annoyers in the stock market.

Morgan detested Gates. He refused to admit him
to the Steel Trust directorate. In return, Gates put

Morgan's Southern Railway in peril. He secretly bought control of Louisville & Nashville. Morgan sent his partner, Perkins, to awaken the Wire King from his slumbers at three o'clock one morning, asking for terms. "Since you want the stock so badly," observed Gates, sleepily rubbing his eyes, "I'll let you have it; but Morgan will have to pay me ten millions more than it cost me." [5]

Morgan closed the deal on the above basis. The Street laughed over his defeat. The great banker suffered a humiliation he never forgot.

Gates pressed his victory. He knew Morgan wanted the Tennessee Coal & Iron Company. Apart from the Trust's Great Northern Ore Lands, that was the most valuable deposit of iron ore in the United States; and it owned two billion tons of coal. Gates formed a pool which bought up the T. C. & I.; he swept the market clean of its shares, and pegged the price. Trading ceased in the stock. So far, so good.

It had been the Wire King's intention to force Morgan to buy the corporation at a high figure. But the Steel Trust pooh-poohed this suggestion, and its heads asserted that they had no use for the property.

Then came the panic of 1907. The Tennessee pool was in a cruel dilemma. It had hypothecated

[5] Carl Hovey: *Life Story of J. Pierpont Morgan.*

its T. C. & I. stock in Wall Street banks. A huge frozen loan of this paper was in the Trust Company of America. The Morgan bankers insisted that the Tennessee loans were a menace to the market, and that they must be removed into strong hands [6]—*i.e.*, into their own.

Hence the order to the Trust Company of America to surrender all its assets to the ruling group.[7]

Morgan had got what he wished. He banished Gates from the Street. The latter never turned another deal. Morgan handed the T. C. & I. over to the Steel Trust. No money was needed—the transaction was accomplished through the simple transfer of securities.[8]

The seal of legitimacy was stamped upon this transaction. The authority of banking opinion in Wall Street, *The Commercial & Financial Chronicle*, says of this episode, in its review of November, 1907: "As part of the plan of relief, and to vitalize certain collateral pledged for loans held by various financial institutions throughout the city, the United States Steel Corporation agreed to purchase a majority of the stock of the Tennessee Coal & Iron Company, agreeing also, on the same terms, to take

[6] *Chronicle*, Jan., 1908, in retrospect of 1907.
[7] *Ibid.*
[8] *Ibid.*

the minority interest. As a preliminary, H. C. Frick and E. H. Gary, had gone on Monday to Washington to assure President Roosevelt that the proposed act would not be an infringement of the Sherman Anti-Trust Law, and apparently got the President to coincide in this view."

It was represented to the President that the sale of the corporation was the only means of putting an end to the panic. In the face of such an argument, Roosevelt surrendered, for there are moments when even the most violent statesmanship succumbs to expediency.

Carl Hovey, in his *Life Story of J. Pierpont Morgan* (a biography approved by the Morgan family), has this to say: "While the panic was still at its height, there came a sudden announcement that the United States Steel Corporation had bought the majority capital stock of the Tennessee Coal & Iron Company. To this day lurks the suspicion that the transaction really explains the panic. It has been made the subject of two Congressional investigations, which uncovered much bad feeling, but failed to dispose of the various charges in a decisive way. It is perhaps still open to any one to think that Morgan deliberately engineered a stupendous financial panic, which was likely to paralyze business, ruin industry, throw his own interests into confusion and set the country back ten years at least, simply to buy at a low price, a stock valued at seventeen million dollars. Those who hold this opinion, support it with the fact that the Tennessee Coal & Iron Company, with its great quantity of ore deposits and its use of the 'open hearth' process for making steel, was an enormously valuable acquisition to the Steel Corporation, and there isn't a doubt that it was. The Steel people asserted at the time of the panic that they didn't want the T. C. & I., and were only taking it over to relieve the situation. But before many months had passed, President Gary, of the Steel Corporation, came out with a statement setting forth the great value in the acquisition of the property. It is fair to conclude that although their first thought was to relieve the strained situation, they were by no means sorry to accomplish this result, with future advantage, rather than future expense to themselves."

This history is written with no intention to criticize such developments: it attempts to be merely a record of human events. In crises, banking is a cruel business: it has to be; and no doubt, the dominant bankers of Wall Street, in their actions taken against the new adventurers and their depositories, as well as in that concerning the T. C. & I., felt themselves justified in safeguarding their banking world, which, as we all must bear in mind, represents also the solvency of our own existence.

This panic had a long aftermath.

Bank failures spread through the country. The Southern Steel Company went bankrupt. The Arnold Print Works was forced to the wall in Massachusetts. The Westinghouse Electric went under in Pittsburgh. Western governors appointed holidays to protect State banks which could not meet their drafts.

One Saturday, Wall Street's Bank Statement showed a loss of thirteen millions cash. Out-of-town banks tried to recall the 800 millions they had on deposit in New York. Then the Street decided to issue Clearing House certificates to prevent the outgo of its specie.

Philadelphia and Pittsburgh locked the doors of their own vaults. Chicago exchange on New York was almost unobtainable. Boston credits in New York were exhausted. The business centers of the country were frozen solid.

Again, as in '93, East Side folk streamed into Wall Street with their little cash hoards, to sell them at a premium. Pay envelopes were filled with silver dollars. The city had gone back to the old cart-wheel coin.

On the morning of November 14, cross-town cars

were rattling through Thirty-fourth Street, their platforms black with clinging passengers. Sidewalks rang with footfalls. Laughing girls, stenographers, dressmakers. Office boys, running or loitering. Porters, grumbling, but hastening their steps. The vast East Side was pouring westward to its taskwork in workrooms and department stores of Fifth Avenue.

Four blocks north, in Park Avenue, a man, still in his nightclothes, was working feverishly over a desk in his bedroom. He was tearing up papers, letters, documents,—destroying them anyhow. He had spent a sleepless night. The troubles of the past month had crashed down upon him. Three-quarters of his fortune had been swept away. Friends, the very ones he had entertained in his luxurious home, whom he had showered with favors, had refused to recognize him in the last few weeks; some of them had spoken of him in terms that had caused him bitter grief.

This man's fingers flexed about the revolver in his desk drawer; then came the explosion; the banker sank slowly to the floor, which he began dyeing with his blood. But before he fired that shot, Barney might have addressed his enemies, and the friends who had deserted and scorned him, in Rousseau's immortal words: "When the final trumpet sounds, and we stand before the throne of the Sovereign Judge, let him among you say, if he dare: '*I was better than that man there!*'"

For, after all, what had been Barney's crime? The Knickerbocker, spoiled in the panic, after an assessment on its stock, and paying the high expenses of receivership, showed, on reopening its doors, assets of fifty-one millions, of which less than thirty-six millions was due to its depositors. The latter were paid in full.[9] Had the company been aided, instead of destroyed, much might have been spared of what afterward became so terrifying and destructive.

No, Barney's crime had been his friendship for a man whom the Street had sworn to destroy.

In January of 1908, those depositories once owned by Heinze, Morse and Thomas, which the Street had supported through the panic period, were permitted to fall into bankruptcy. The National Bank of North America, the New Amsterdam National, the Mechanics' & Traders', the Oriental, lost their corporate identities; their business was absorbed by the dominant group.[10]

Resentment may slumber, it rarely dies. On information supplied by the Street, expert accountants set to work upon books of banks involved in the late

[9] *Herald*, March 27, 1908.
[10] *Ibid.*, Jan. 27-31, 1908.

unpleasantness; they searched for violations of banking laws.

Successful men rarely fear such inquisitions. The losers, the defeated, always pay.

These proceedings were aimed at Heinze, Morse and Thomas,—but the indictment papers of a fourth, potential criminal, were left blank; he was out of reach of man's punishment.

Thomas defeated the intentions of his enemies; he sold his villa, his racing studs, and turned over to Wall Street a part of his income.

Heinze, also, was indicted, but afterward cleared from blame; his wealth mostly gone, he tried to recoup in Montana; but his entanglements kept him in litigations, inextricable, complicated, interminable, spun on for years and ending only in the bold miner's death.

Morse was sent to Federal prison. Barney had been driven to suicide. The mills of Wall Street had ground exceeding fine.

Most of the principals who performed the parts of culprits in the stageplay are now dead: Heinze, Thomas, Barney. As for the heroes, the great victors, Rogers, the business genius, William Rockefeller, who so loved speculation, Stillman, the implacable, the elder Morgan, so proud,—they, too, have passed away.

XXX

E VERY panic has to have its presidential scape-
goat; in '37, he was Andrew Jackson; in '93,
it was Grover Cleveland; in 1907, men spoke of the
"Roosevelt Panic"; but the Roughrider had as little
to do with the matter as had Mr. Hoover with the
events of 1929, although probably these will live in
memory as the "Hoover Panic."

Roosevelt's political formulas sprang from the
events of his time: the monopolies of '93, the later
industrial combinations, the dismal fate of the "Shipping Trust." This vigorous personality wished to
limit large fortunes; he uttered startling pronounce-
ments; such as "If righteousness conflicts with the
fancied needs of business, then the latter must go to
the wall!" [1] This is strange stuff for present-day
ears.

Roosevelt was a provocative figure, no doubt,
while Wall Street was wracked by its bank runs; but
this man's tremendous "policies" had certainly not
set the Street's destructive machinery in motion.

[1] *Chronicle*, Jan., 1908, in retrospect of 1907.

The catastrophe of 1907 did not travel the classic route. In the long continuity of its troubles, the numerity of its principals, its theatrical effects, it eclipses the intermediate conjunctures; in importance it overshadows all the rest.

In 1901, there was a dispute between financiers: a moneyed intrigue, involved, mysterious; its complexities have no parallel in modern times.

But the events of 1907 were amazingly simple; one follows them without effort: two high financiers, held up by an adventurous miner; their capitulation; Heinze's bold ambitions; the league of the banker-adventurers,—Heinze, Morse, Thomas, Barney; the dominant group threatened in their hegemony; waiting for a weak link in the armor of their rivals; taking advantage of the cracking of the United Copper corner. Public fright. The plight of the Morgan group, when its own world was set rocking; the selection of a sacrifice in the shape of a trust company, upon which to hurl the wrath of panic.

There's scarcely room for argument here. The panic of 1907, above all other panics, was the result of men's manipulations. Let us abandon economic subterfuges, for these facts are plain, simple, indisputable.

So ended our greatest of panics. Did it teach Wall Street a lasting lesson?

Why, not at all.

The sordid ending of the inflations of 1929 is still ringing in our ears: exposures of forgeries, failures, suicides, aborted pools; false faith in investment trusts.

And what is going to be done about it? Shall we continue to indulge in ponderous considerations of the old economic tomfooleries; contemplate the restriction of brokers' loans; but why not restrict activities of the men who make them?

IX

THE MEN WHO MAKE PANICS

XXXI

THE MEN WHO MAKE PANICS

IN scanning the men who influenced the financial convulsions of a century of yesterdays, and those who had to do with the one that trailed its dismaying consequences through the days of 1930, one is struck by a great diversity and multiformity of characters. Here were very practical minds, with vivid understanding of the present, and correct vision of the future; there were zealous promoters among them, gifted with energy and imagination; explorers, also, plunging blindly along venturesome highways; there were some who built lasting and substantial things, while others were creatures of fancy and delusion; and always, in the background, slunk the mob of camp-followers, made up of tricksters, sly wolves and scrubby rascals.

And when one is called to sound the problem of all their press of business, the answer should not seem so very difficult, if one regards the happening of panic, not as a catastrophe, necessarily,[1] but as a phase of evolution in which nature works its way. A few

[1] Burton: *Financial Crises.*

generations ago, the slant-eyed soldiers pillaging the Yangtse Valley in China's civil war, were armed with sham weapons and hid behind paper forts; but in our time, when rifles and machine guns fell into their hands, they began to destroy outworn forms, old habits and ancient, moldering cities, and so they became a constructive force.

Some analogy suggests itself in a contemplation of the cycle that ends in panic. The men of the thirties taught a useful lesson to their thirteen million countrymen, who were called upon to master a continent; the florid infatuations of Biddle, the rashness of the Josephs brothers, proved that that conquest could not be accomplished by such crude and dangerous expedients as selling State bonds—afterwards defaulted—to bolster up speculations in cotton, building visionary towns and establishing shaky banks in the wilderness.

In the fifties, when adventurers began the development of the Greater West beyond the Alleghanies, those who remained behind to gamble on the prospects of their fellows,—short-sighted bankers, and even jugglers and forgers like Schuyler and Kyle, served to disclose the disabilities of the times, the financial weakness which could not support all this advancement, resulting in currency inflation and the siphoning of gold from the country; and, in consequence, a long string of ruined depositories brought about the adoption of National Banking laws.

Then those forty million people in '73, stimulated by the progressive forces of opportunism, who saw promoters building their thirty-thousand miles of railway, in shadowy outlines beyond the Rockies, precariously, by Jay Cooke with his Northern Pacific, dishonestly, by Oakes Ames and his Crédit Mobilier; they witnessed the waste and destruction which succeeded in the default of seventy-two railroads; these lessons resulted in preventive legislation, the warranty of betterment; for as Clément Juglar, the Frenchman, reminded the world of his time, the regular development of the riches of nations does not take place without suffering or without resistance.[2]

In the eighties came a still more convincing forward movement: telegraph companies established, land development renewed, railroads now in competition; but the teachers were a shabbier lot: projectors, like Seney, wreckers of the Eno type, dealers in delusions, like Ferdinand Ward, tricksters, like that agile money-lender, Sage; but behind the smoke-screen of their thefts, defalcations and impositions, they demonstrated afresh the penalties of imprudence by

[2] Clément Juglar: *Des Crises Commerciales, et De Leur Retour Périodique,* Paris, 1889.

casting into relief the stupid gullibility of the confiding and the over-credulous.

The mystery of panic is still more understandable in the events of '93, if one entertains them as evidences of a driving power that impelled the men of that time to lay the cornerstones of industry; even though, in doing so, they attempted to monopolize the assets of a country of seventy millions; for those over-confident contrivers, James M. Waterbury and A. A. McLeod, exhibited the fallacy of creating trusts with the aim of raising prices and keeping them raised.

Does this view hold good with the men of the twentieth century, Hill and Harriman, those profound plotters, building railroads into still remoter territories, with a better knowledge than their predecessors of what those highways meant? Yes, the analogy persists, because speculation, adventure, intrigue, are characteristics of an energetic people; and those financiers and their bankers, playing checkmate with one another, bringing the moneyed and speculative worlds to the point of ruin, unconsciously indicated the necessity for correcting such operations as theirs, and gave a firmer foundation to efforts already begun, to impose National and State control upon railway management.

In 1907 one again encounters the agents of a forward movement: Morgan, Stillman, Rogers, Heinze, Morse; developers of steel and copper industries, of shipping companies, manipulators of banking combinations; it was progress through the instrumentality of the same old human elements, more prodigal in method than formerly, more remorseless in execution; but by their bank wars, their copper pools, their insecure shipping mergers, they threw the financial world into such hazardous tumult, that the Federal Reserve System was established in consequence.[3]

Can any one who looks for the causal factors in the panics of '93, 1901, 1907 and 1929, seriously believe that these were not the results of men's manipulations, but that they were derived from some undetermined economic features? That the flight of gold, the currency inflations of '37 and '57, were not consequences of human action?

In 1930 we were confronted with overproduction, —of wheat, cotton, silks, textiles; how evident it is to our eyes that this condition was due to excessive emissions of capital by optimistic corporate promotions. Overproduction—aside from the incident of copper cornering—was absent in our greater panic of 1907, absent also in 1901 and '93; but stress is laid to-day also on complexities in modern business life, over-

[3] See Carter Glass: *An Adventure in Constructive Finance,* 1927.

277

stimulation of loans, overextension of credits, as though such developments were not palpable results of man's handiwork; in the past, the chief emphasis was laid on crop failure; even so careful a financial student as Charles A. Conant ascribes England's panic of 1847 to the crop failure in Ireland; [4] yet it needs no close study to discover that that event was caused by unwise railway builders, who, by April of that year, had committed their country to expenditures of not less than £130,000,000 by their promotions.[5] And crop variations have had but a small part in effecting panics: before the panic of '84, grain crops were even larger than those of '82,[6] and crop failure was distinctly absent in the convulsions of 1907 [7] and 1929. *The explanation of panics must show some factor that is common to them all,* and in those which we have contemplated in Wall Street's history, they have uniformly revealed themselves as the results of human schemes and human undertakings.

When we come to our own time, in 1929, we witness real progress overshadowed by the same ill-timed undertakings, by sordid examples of deception and rascality; by the acts of super-optimists, typified

[4] Conant: *History of Modern Banks of Issue.*
[5] London *Economist,* April 10, 1847.
[6] Noyes: *Forty Years of American Finance.*
[7] *Chronicle,* January, 1908, in retrospect of 1907.

in the organizers of imprudent investment trusts, bank affiliates, bank chains; by stock market quacks, by cheats in motor accessory, farm implement, airplane and radio shares; by that pool with its Ford contract hoax; and these actions manifest the age-old story of the waste and destruction of capital by speculative quackeries; by reckless prodigalities, by destructive extravagance; accentuated by the childish philosophies of impractical economists. All this, however, again obscured a background of real achievement, many new enterprises born: utilities, air navigation, radio and motor enterprises.

It was a new era, indeed, but not that era described by the financial philosophers; not a new era for bamboozled buyers of the maddening flood of common stocks, inflated, split-up, paid out as bonuses to bankers, distributed as dividends, or paid in salaries. Those from whom the capital was drawn for all the advancement represented by the inflations of 1929, occupy the place that all such folk have occupied periodically since the days of '37: they paid the piper and were left with empty pockets.

From all this one may be entitled to reason that the panic is not actually a catastrophe, but that it represents a check in a forward movement; it has spurred men of energy and foresight on into shaping the future; but such men, only too often, through miscalculation, errors and even by design, concert in the dissipation of hoarded capital, the exploitation of the unsuspecting many; in miscarriage, misfortune and disaster.[8] *Men do not make panics deliberately; they are their unconscious agents.*

In the moment of downfall and discomfiture, one cannot afford to sit back complacently, like the professor of economy, and conclude of the panic of 1929: "The slump in stock prices destroyed no physical assets. It was found that, to a large extent, the crash in prices had robbed thousands of Peters to pay a very few Pauls." Such shabby philosophy doesn't fit into present-day ideas; it is dangerous, indeed, at a time when our friends beyond the Urals seem to think that the capitalist himself is on probation, and capitalism is more or less on trial. Why should it not be our accountability to prove that their theories are wrong?

Wise generations take advantage of such moments as those brought into relief by the disturbances of 1929; they revise themselves, in order to become stronger and safer. Behind our forward movement, behind the panic of yesterday, lies the highly elaborated machinery of Wall Street; admirable as it is in theory, and quite ordinarily in practice, this gigantically developed apparatus was misused in a great cataclysm by powerful marketeers, who utilized it in

[8] See Burton: *Financial Crises*, summary and conclusion.

seizing upon the country's accumulated money through the Federal Reserve,[9] to destroy the growing prosperity, to exploit the millions of newly-born investors which that prosperity had brought about, on a grander scale than ever before, to spur speculation through those agencies which our modern progress has produced: designing publicity, expert salesmanship, the radio.

It may be that in our generation, with its advanced wisdom, the coming of panic can be prevented, as our haruspices so confidently assure us; but if not, then at least, its worst features should be controlled: waste of competence, cruelties of exploitation.

Can that be done? Can the imperfections in the Street's machinery be corrected?

That is the true problem that faces the proposed investigators, who are called upon to delve into the causes that led to the convulsion of 1929.

[9] "The Reserve Banks, by their policy, aided Stock Exchange speculation indirectly, but they never do this directly." *Chronicle*, Jan.-March, 1928, p. 286.

XXXII

SO it was fair wisdom in Senator Burton to warn those who study panics not to "confuse effects with cause, and mistake what is subordinate or incidental, for the principal fact." For if all cycles of progress are motivated by men whose actions lead to panic, why, then the travail of our Federal inquirers isn't to devise means to avoid high money rates, limit loans on Stock Exchange collateral, and the like, but to make the country safe for its investors, by frustrating a reappearance of such extravagance as was witnessed in the period ending in the autumn of '29.

Mr. Hoover's Committee on Recent Economic Changes, early in 1929, admitted that immunity from serious trade depression since 1921 had encouraged optimists to predict that the business cycle had been ironed out in the United States. One would be but too willing to give credence to the seers and soothsayers, had they not so often cozened us in the past. In the sixties, men believed that the National Banking System had at last prevented a return of such catastrophes as those of '37 and '57; anticipating the

282

arrival of 1907, bankers professed that the days of
'73, '84 and '93 could never be repeated; then, in consequence of the great panic of that year, the Federal
Reserve System was created, primarily to circumvent
such cyclical upheavals in the future. But once more
the world was deluded, as the occurrences of 1929
bear witness.

A doubt suggests itself whether the collapse of
1929 was actually entitled to the term of "major
panic"; a mere stock market breakdown does not con-
stitute one, while conspicuously absent was the "precipitating cause," the initial indication of all true
panics. In '37, the precipitating cause was the failure
of the Josephs brothers banking house; in '57, it was
the closing of the Ohio Life Insurance & Trust Company; in '73, it was the downfall of Jay Cooke; in
'84, the exposure of Grant & Ward; in '93, the collapse of the Cordage Trust; in 1901, the corner that
eventuated in Northern Pacific; in 1907, it was the
frustration of Heinze's United Copper pool.

But the nose-dive in market values came in 1929
without the blazoning of any big failure, although in
the seclusion of banking parlors there were known to
be embarrassments a-plenty; nor were there any of
those desperate bank runs of the past. The exemp-
tion from such calamitous events may be explained
in that we, having outgrown our debtor nation stature

283

of former days, no longer suffer from the lack of liquid funds; and the Federal Reserve, in strengthening bank resources, and providing a more equal distribution of capital in crises, has justified the advantages of its existence.[1]

But, alas, all this was small consolation; for the débâcle came, notwithstanding, and ushered in the most formidable market downfall in history, the highest losses ever inflicted upon the people of any country through the irresponsibilities of those who manage its financial world. Calamities so long drawn out, that one year later, toward the close of 1930, came suspensions of great Stock Exchange wire houses, that had sponsored investment trusts and company flotations, and had been carried along for twelve months by their bankers in a vain effort to save them. The fear is well-founded that if the future operations of the Street's vast mechanism are not constrained, other and even more costly ordeals may come to plague us.

Our attorney general's officers periodically impress us with the appalling hundreds of millions in impost with which bucket shop bounders and schemers in spurious stocks annually assess the country; but such impositions shrink into the pale of nothingness when contrasted with the billions in impaired values with

[1] Carter Glass: *An Adventure in Constructive Finance*, 1927.

which ingenious experts in finance taxed the popula-
tion of the United States through the medium of the
Stock Exchange in 1929. Students of a serious type
were unwitting to the approach of that convulsion of
'29; they were the chart men, the inductive economists, the tape readers and other financial astrologers;
industrious professors of Yale and Harvard may pore
solemnly over their "index numbers," but these have
exactly the same relative importance as the "past performances" of track favorites in the columns of the
sports page.

These gentlemen, with their university courses in
unwise finance, assumed much responsibility for what
happened; they lectured the average citizen to fly
from bonds and preferred shares to common stocks,—
those common stocks poured out in superfluous abandon, paid by corporations as salaries to their officers,
as dividends to their stockholders, as bonuses to their
bankers, their brokers, their underwriters, and as commissions to their stock drummers. What became of
those common stock values was only too forcibly
demonstrated in the closing months of 1930; the
falsity of such teachings was palpable; for the more
stock issued, the less is the value of that outstanding;
because, when the public demand lessens for that
commodity, as values shrink, and losses pile up, practical financiers promptly issue preferred stocks, that

285

take precedence of the common as to assets,—and that is precisely what was subsequently illustrated in the corporate annals of the Street.

Those highly capable and far-sighted industrial captains from the Middle West, who gave their dinner of jubilation at the Biltmore, had for previous years been busied laudably in promoting or building up large and prosperous new industries; [2] in those days of their triumphs, strong weapons fell into their hands, and, since they were but human, they could not withstand the temptation to use them; they were fortunate in being able to utilize the capital of the country and the machinery provided for its distribution.

What was behind their junket, which was to transform it into a Feast of the Barmecides for the balance of their countrymen? They boasted that they had driven Radio up to $500 a share; but in 1930, only a few months after the market's downfall, that corporation disclosed that it had not earned dividends even on its preferred shares, and therefore nothing on the common that had been so jubilantly accelerated in its quotations; they prided themselves that similarly they had elevated "with their golden touch," General Motors, International Harvester, American International, Anaconda, International Nickel and Cast Iron

[2] Earl Sparling: *Mystery Men of Wall Street.*

286

Pipe; [3] yet it was but a comparatively short time after, that many of the corporations responsible for these securities, became conspicuous in the closing of their mines, the shutting down of industrial plants, in the discharge of their workmen, the reduction or the passing of their dividends, and the phenomenal losses in the market value of their outstanding paper. He who runs may read the consequences of these "past performances" in the financial columns of his daily newspaper. These gentlemen had upset the realities of life for a lot of persons, themselves included.

Too much of the foregoing represents little in consonance with our practical revisions of business life, our views of equity, even of common sense. In such ways of obtaining investors' funds, by exchanging securities for their money, there's a smack of obsolescence, in their deceptive assumptions, insincerities and subterfuges. But the remedy seems to lie close at hand,—an opportunity for our Federal investigators to acknowledge and correct those faulty, outworn, outdated mechanisms in Wall Street's machinery. A Federal-controlled Wall Street,—does that sound so remote? Nearer, perhaps than it sounds, for, being admittedly engaged in interstate commerce, and not an incorporated State body, the

[3] N. Y. Times, April 20, 1928, p. 25.

Stock Exchange, at least, is susceptible to Government regulation.

Were these investigators—having the authority—to examine the books of the large commission and wire houses of the Street, they might cogitate the principle which enables 98 per cent of margin traders to be done out of their deposits,—a process pursued week upon week, month after month, year upon end, leading to no useful purpose, providing capital for no new enterprise. It merely keeps oiled the perpetual mechanism of the Street; the funds devoured in this process go in part to augment the beehives of industrious brokers; to build up the imposing bank palaces of the Street,—but we could dispense with some of that splendor. Besides, what sort of business is this, which allures its clients by not the most upright of inducements, dissipates their substance, and leaves them with angry minds and empty hands,—a business whose clockwork is suddenly magnified on occasions to terrifying proportions, such as we witnessed in the excited inflations of '29, with demoralized, improvident and uneconomic consequences.[4]

A scrutiny might prove profitable, also, of those more exclusive houses, the rendezvous of influence and abundant means, which indulge their clients in the pastime of concocting pools and corners; the Ex-

[4] See Stedman: *N. Y. Stock Exchange.*

change might be persuaded to levy the threat of expulsion upon firms permitting such manipulations. Our big operator, to be sure, affects the attitude that his market practices are his private concern; hidden in seclusion, the aristocratic plunderer sees the harvest he reaps, but is spared the sight of the miseries of those from whom he draws his profits,—such miseries as were so numerously exhibited in the autumn days of '29.

In fact, our generation has perhaps outgrown the fashions now maintained by habit, custom, maybe general consent, in raising its capital; changes in these modes should be salutary to all concerned; the Street's underwriting banks are too indispensable for us to permit their officers again to encourage speculations through their newly conceived securities affiliates; its commission men are too efficient as agents in disseminating paper wealth for us to agree to their methods of legerdemain in handling listed shares and bond certificates, until they fall, too often diminished in value, into the hands of final investors; the Stock Exchange, itself, is too serviceable to the country as a distributor of capital, for the offices of its members to be utilized as a medium for chicane and misrepresentation; [5] in effect, the entire instrumentality of the

---

[5] See *Function of the Stock Exchange*, by Matthew Marshall, in introduction to *New York Stock Exchange*, by Stedman.

Street is too requisite for the circulation and distribution of our moneyed wealth, for it to be misused as a leverage in the disorganization and extinction of the common capital of the people.

Surely, such requisitions should not be regarded as unreasonable. The small merchant who misrepresents his wares, is made to feel his moral and legal responsibility in short order by our Better Business Bureaus; such being the accepted rule in the commercial world, why shouldn't it prevail in financial life? And, to sum up, that is what's wrong with Wall Street.

Incidentally, it should prove instructive to ask to the witness stand those diners who celebrated their market victories at the famous dinner at the Biltmore; to question them whether they actually believed they were creating real values by marking up the market prices of their stocks.

There still remains the sanguine expectation that we may end by ironing out our business cycles; if, in the dormancy of the panic, there is really a progressive force, and we naturally desire to remain a progressive people, it is imperative for us to control its tendencies toward unthriftiness and improvidence, to minimize its casualties and extinguish its catastrophic features; to accomplish this, it is necessary to revise the prevalent irresponsibility in marketing securities;

to write *finis* to the prodigal ways of soliciting investments; to persuade promoters and underwriters of
corporations to a consciousness of greater accountability toward those from whom they ask financial
coöperation.

For a century we have attempted to retrieve the
destructive influences of panics; their indicia have
been gathered diligently by economic professors; but
the latter appear mistakenly to have studied effects
and not causes; we have devised the Clearing House,
the National Banking Law, the Federal Reserve, but
invariably the wits and energies of the men whose
activities lead to panics have circumvented such preventive measures, by playing with the accumulated
property which thrift gathered, worked for and
saved.

The study of one hundred years of financial convulsions has shown us quite plainly that they do not
spend their wrath upon us because there chance to be
fewer fruiting spikes in the farmer's wheat field; or
because some have produced more goods than they
can sell, or business men have borrowed too much,
and meet defeat when they can borrow no longer;
but that panics represent something that is as old as
human illusion; that false optimisms are more per-
nicious than lack of faith; and that if we fail in
marching abreast of amendment, by checking, at

periods of exceptional activity, the unwise promotion, the disastrous speculation, and the demoralizing fraud which invariably accompany them, and that if we are neither strong nor wise enough to stem the waste in accumulating investment capital, which is at the bottom of all such upheavals, we shall not succeed in placing an end to the calamities of panics—never—never—

"Until the axle break
That keeps the stars in their round,
And hands hurl in the deep
The banners of East and West,
And the girdle of light is unbound."

INDEX

INDEX

Adler, Dr. Cyrus, 189, 190, 198, 218

Allen, Henry, Cordage Trust speculation, 159; fails, 164

Amalgamated Copper Company, organized by Henry H. Rogers, 223; launched by National City Bank, 223; financed by J. P. Morgan & Co., 223; shares crash, 224; war with Heinze, 226, 227; buys his properties, 227

American Exchange Bank, "run" on in 1857, 88

American Ice Company, organized by Charles W. Morse, 227, 228; shares crash in Panic of 1907, 233

American International shares, their price boosted by the "Western Giants," 18; shares collapse, 30, 287

Ames, Oakes, one of promoters of Union Pacific, 99; expelled from House, fails for eight millions, 100

Anaconda shares, price boosted by the "Western Giants," 18; shares collapse, 30, 287

Anti-Trust Law, Northern Securities Company held to be violation of, 217; Tennessee Coal & Iron deal held not to be violation of, 260-262

Arnold Print Works forced to wall, 263

Aspinwall (now Colon), gold fleets steam to Port of New York from, 74, 82

Atchison Railroad, receivership, 176

Atchison shares, price drop in 1901, 213

Atlantic Bank, broken in 1873, 101

Bacon, Robert, of J. P. Morgan & Company, confers with Hill and Perkins on N.P. situation, 196; notifies them of Morgan's cablegram, 199; financiers warn him, 214; one of bankers dominating Wall Street in 1907, 230

Baker, George F., banker, forms money pool with Stillman and Morgan to save brokers in 1907, 230

Bank of Commerce, "run" on in 1857, 85

Bank of the Commonwealth, closed in Panic of 1873, 107

Bank of New Amsterdam, bought by Morse, 228; "run" on, 234; supported by Clearing House through Panic of 1907, 235; bankrupt and absorbed by dominant group at close of panic, 265

Bank of New York, organized by Alexander Hamilton, 56; under its leadership, Whigs

297

INDEX

New Era theories, 10, 20; their blindness to the coming panic, 285

Chemical Bank, pays gold, 88

Chicago fire, in 1871, 99

Chicago & Mississippi Railroad, 77

Clark, Dodge & Company, downed in Panic of 1857, 85

Clearing House, then situated over Bank of New York, issues ten millions in certificates during Panic of 1873, 107; scene in the, during Grant & Ward Panic, 130; issues loan certificates in Panic of 1893, 168; actions taken by its Association during Panic of 1907, 233-236; issues certificates in Panic of 1907, 263

Cleveland, President Grover, signs repeal of silver purchase bill, 175; blamed for Panic of 1893, 267

Clews, Henry, suspends in Panic of 1873, 107

Coal Company, Parker Vein, officials of flood stock market with fraudulent share issue, 77

Commercial & Financial Chronicle, banking authority of Wall Street; its comment on Tennessee Coal & Iron deal, 260, 261

Consolidated Bank, bought by Heinze, 229; supported through Panic of 1907 by Clearing House, 234

Cooke, Jay, his appearance; his position as a banker, 97; his promotion of Northern Pacific, 98; closes his historic firm, 102; his downfall, 103; scenes at his Wall Street banking house, 104; vanishes from existence as a firm, 108; recovers fortune, and regains possession of country-place, 111-113

Cordage Trust, founded, 155, 156; its shares boom, 159; downfall of, 161-165

"Corners" — Nicholas Biddle corners world's cotton, 52; Northern Pacific cornered in 1901, 206; Heinze's United Copper corner, in 1907, 232

Cortelyou, George B., Secretary of Treasury, watches mob from Sub-Treasury; rushes orders to Washington for twenty-five millions, 255, 256

Cottonseed Oil Trust, one of monopolies of 1893, 153

Crédit Mobilier, organized by promoters of Union Pacific, 99; overwhelmed by scandal, 100

Deacon, "Charley," veteran doorkeeper of Stock Exchange, 164

"Deacon" (the Hon. Stephen) White, stock operator; Lackawanna deal, in '84; Whiskey Trust deal in '92; Cordage Trust deal in '93, 157; caught in Cordage smash; his suspension; compromises with creditors; resumes seat on 'Change, 166, 167

Denver & Rio Grande Railroad,

298

INDEX

Hatch, Daniel B., partner of Hatch & Foote, 136, 137
Hatch & Foote, suspend in Panic of 1884, 137
Heinsheimer, partner of Jacob H. Schiff, 202; distresses Harriman, 203
Henriques, Moses, joins Josephs Brothers banking house, 55; broken in Panic of 1837, 67, 68
Heinze, Arthur, brother of F. Augustus, 226
Heinze, F. Augustus, his fight with Amalgamated, 225, 226; joins Morse in Wall Street, 227; president of banks, 229; his copper corner broken, 232, 233; forced to resign, 234; his death, 266
Heinze, Otto & Company, brokerage house fails, 232, 233
Herzfeld & Stern, Kuhn, Loeb brokers, 200
Higgins, A. Foster, succeeds Charles T. Barney as head of Knickerbocker Trust, 239; interviews Morgan, 240
Hill, James Jerome, appearance, characteristics; builds Great Northern Railroad, 185; contest with Harriman, 186-193; discovers Harriman's plot, 195-198; joins Morgan in Northern Pacific imbroglio, 199
Holding companies, railroad, how organized, 19; disappoint investors, 32
Hollins, "Harry" B., director of Knickerbocker Trust; de-

mands resignation of Charles T. Barney, 236
Hoover, President Herbert, his Committee on Recent Economic Changes, 282; unjust accusation of the "Hoover Panic," 267
Horn Silver Mine, Jay Cooke's last enterprise, 112, 113
Hotchkiss & Burnham, fail in Grant & Ward Panic, 135
Hovey, Carl, 184, 218, 236, 237, 245, 246, 247, 255, 259, 261, 262
Howland Thomas, defaulter, 80
Huntington, Collis P., merchant adventurer in the fifties, 73

Indianapolis, word from that there is scarcely a dollar in Indiana save free bank paper, 81
Investment trusts, discovery of the college professors regarding them, 19; dismal consequences of their theory, 31
International Harvester shares, their inflation by the "Western Giants," 18; their collapse, 286, 287
International Mercantile Marine, organized by J. Pierpont Morgan, 184

Jackson, President Andrew, war upon Second Bank of the United States, 52, 53
Jarvis-Conklin Mortgage Trust Company, in receivership in Panic of 1893, 166   [57
Jauncey, Mr., his stylish home, Jersey Central Railroad, in Mc-

302

303

INDEX

Market Bank, looted, 80;
broken, 87
McGuigan, steals $50,000 from
Ocean Bank, 80
Mechanics' Bank, "run" upon in
1837, 61
Mechanics' Banking Association, fails, 85
Mechanics' & Traders' Bank,
owned by E. R. Thomas, 229
McLeod, A. A., his anthracite
monopoly, 154, 155; its defeat, 176
Mercantile National Bank,
headed by F. A. Heinze, 229;
supported through Panic of
1907 on condition of his resignation, 234
Merchant, greatest American,
trusteed in 1907, 25
Merchants' Exchange, destroyed
by fire, 57; new, in Panic of
1857, 88; its lofty colonnade,
36
Merger, example of wire-screen,
10, 11, 12; its dénouement,
24, 25, 26
Metropolitan Bank, "run" on,
85; its action against John
Thompson, 90; Seney its
president, 118; closed, 134,
135
Microphone, utilized in stock
selling, 20
Mills, bank president, drowned,
101
Mills, Darius O., merchant adventurer, 73
Mills, John, political economist,
41
Minnie Healy, a Heinze mine,
226

Missouri, Kansas & Texas
Railroad, unable to meet its
loans, 100
Mobile, merchants suspend, 61
Moore, Prof. Henry Ludwell,
42
Moore & Schley, brokers, 209
Monopolies, of 1893, 153-155;
their downfall, 165
Morgan, Henry, 121, 122; fails,
136
Morgan, J. Pierpont, arrives in
Wall Street, 183; his appearance in 1901, 183; his promotions, 184; sails abroad, 195;
historic cablegram, 199; re-
turns from South, 235; re-
fuses to aid Knickerbocker
Trust, 240; his appearance at
seventy, 244; his game of
"Louis," 244, 245; his library,
245; his conference there,
246-251; his plan developed,
258; opposes Gates, 258; buys
L. & N. from him, 259; ban-
ishes Gates from Street, 260;
his death, 266
Morgan Line of steamers, 187
Morgan's Sons, Matthew, 121,
136
Morris, Gouverneur, fails, 79,
80
Morse, Charles W., his corporations, 227, 228; his bank purchases, 228; his associations,
229; his loans called, 233;
forced to resign from his
banks, 234, 235; sent to Federal prison, 266
Motion picture audiences, educated to buy stocks through
movietone, 20

304

Oberholtzer, Ellis Paxon, 97, 102, 103, 111-113
O'Brien, bonanza king, 73
Ocean Bank, broken in Panic of 1857, 87
"Ogontz," country-place of Jay Cooke, 102, 113
Ohio Central Railroad, controlled by Seney Syndicate, 118
Ohio Life Insurance & Trust Company, its failure, 83, 84
Opdyke, George, president of N. Y. & Oswego Midland Railroad, suspends, 104, 105
Oriental Bank, controlled by Morse-Heinze-Thomas group; supported through Panic of 1907 by Clearing House; bankrupted at end of panic and absorbed by dominant group, 265
Orton, Sir Roger, his comments on men with money and men with brains, 46

Panic, of 1837, 59-65; of 1847 (in Europe), 278; of 1857, 83-88; of 1873, 102-108; of 1884, 132-138; of 1893, 160-176; of 1901, 206-216; of 1907, 232-266; of 1929, 22-33
"Panic birds," first seen in Wall Street, 144, 145
Panics, their causal factors, 277
Panics, men who make, 273-281
Panics, study of, 38-47
Patterson, Dr. E. M., quotation from his lecture, 41
Paul, William, Belmont's cashier, 80

Perkins, George W., Morgan's partner, 196, 199, 237, 255
Philadelphia, stronghold of American finance in 1837, 51, 52
Philadelphia & Reading Railroad, A. A. McLeod president of, 155; his operations through its shares, 175, 176; Reading receivership, 176
Pigou, political economist, 41
"Plunger," his tactics in Panic of 1893, 170-174
Produce Exchange, Stock Exchange brokers use floor of, 206
Produce Exchange Bank, bought by Morse, 228
Pyle, Joseph Gilpin, 185, 186, 187, 195, 196, 198, 199, 200, 217, 218

Radio, how utilized in selling stock, 14, 15, 20, 21; its result, 34
Railroad holding companies, how organized, 19; loss to investors, 32
"Regular bids," their significance in Panic of 1901, 211
Robinson, Nelson & Company, 119; fail, 134
Rochester & Pittsburg Railroad, controlled by Seney Syndicate, 118
Rock Island shares, their price drop in 1901, 213.
Rockefeller, William, 230, 266
Rogers, Henry H., 223, 225, 266
Rogers, Isaiah, builder of Merchants' Exchange, later the Custom House, now remod-

306

309

INDEX

310

Lightning Source UK Ltd.
Milton Keynes UK
UKHW011135180320
360547UK00001B/299